THE JOY OF WORSHIP

LIBRARY OF LIVING FAITH

John M. Mulder, General Editor

THE JOY
OF
WORSHIP

BY

MARIANNE H. MICKS

THE WESTMINSTER PRESS
PHILADELPHIA

241. 36
M 583

BOOK DESIGN BY DOROTHY ALDEN SMITH

82090331

First edition

Published by The Westminster Press®
Philadelphia, Pennsylvania

PRINTED IN THE UNITED STATES OF AMERICA
9 8 7 6 5 4 3 2 1

Library of Congress Cataloging in Publication Data

Micks, Marianne H.
  The joy of worship.

  (Library of living faith)
  Bibliography: p.
  1. God—Worship and love. 2. Public worship.
3. Prayer. I. Title. II. Series.
BV4817.M5   248.3   81–19667
ISBN 0–664–24402–5   AACR2

CONTENTS

FOREWORD

The word "theology" comes from two Greek words—
theos ("God") and *logos* ("word" or "thought"). Theology
is simply words about God or thinking about God. But for
many Christians, theology is remote, abstract, baffling,
confusing, and boring. They turn it over to the profession-
als—the theologians—who can ponder and inquire into
the ways of God with the world.

This series, Library of Living Faith, is for those Christians who thought theology wasn't for them. It is a collection of ten books on crucial doctrines or issues in the Christian faith today. Each book attempts to show why our
theology—our thoughts about God—matters in what we
do and say as Christians. The series is an invitation to
readers to become theologians themselves—to reflect on
the Bible and on the history of the church and to find their
own ways of understanding the grace of God in Jesus
Christ.

The Library of Living Faith is in the tradition of another
series published by Westminster Press in the 1950s, the
Layman's Theological Library. This new collection of
volumes tries to serve the church in the challenges of the
closing decades of this century.

The ten books are based on the affirmation of the Letter
to the Ephesians (4:4–6): "There is one body and one

Spirit, just as you were called to the one hope that belongs
to your call, one Lord, one faith, one baptism, one God and
Father of us all, who is above all and through all and in all."
Each book addresses a particular theme as' part of the
Christian faith as a whole; each book speaks to the church
as a whole. Theology is too important to be left only to the
theologians; it is the work and witness of the entire people
of God.

But, as Ephesians says, "grace was given to each of us
according to the measure of Christ's gift" (Eph. 4:7), and
the Library of Living Faith tries to demonstrate the diversity of theology in the church today. Differences, of course,
are not unique to American Christianity. One only needs
to look at the New Testament and the early church to see
how "the measure of Christ's gift" produced disagreement
and conflict as well as a rich variety of understandings of
Christian faith and discipleship. In the midst of the unity
of the faith, there has never been uniformity. The authors
in this series have their own points of view, and readers
may argue along the way with the authors' interpreta-
tions. But each book presents varying points of view and
shows what difference it makes to take a particular theological position. Sparks may fly, but the result, we hope,
will be a renewed vision of what it means to be a Christian
exhibiting in the world today a living faith.

These books are also intended to be a library—a set of
books that should be read together. Of course, not everything is included. As the Gospel of John puts it, "There are
also many other things which Jesus did; were every one of
them to be written I suppose that the world itself could not
contain the books that would be written" (John 21:25).
Readers should not be content to read just the volume on
Jesus Christ or on God or on the Holy Spirit and leave out
those on the church or on the Christian life or on Christianity's relationship with other faiths. For we are called to
one faith with many parts.

The volumes are also designed to be read by groups of people. Writing may be a lonely task, but the literature of the church was never intended for individuals alone. It is for the entire body of Christ. Through discussion and even debate, the outlines of a living faith can emerge.

The psalmist declared, "I was glad when they said to me, 'Let us go to the house of the LORD!' " (Ps. 122:1). Marianne H. Micks recovers this sense of gladness in describing *the joy of worship.* As she demonstrates, worship is not simply what we do in church but is the heart of how we live our lives as Christians each day.

Dr. Micks is professor of biblical and historical theology at Virginia Theological Seminary. She served as a campus minister for the Episcopal Church at Smith College and at the University of California at Berkeley and is the author of *Introduction to Theology* (1964), *The Future Present: The Phenomenon of Christian Worship* (1970), as well as other books and articles. She has long been a student of the history and theology of Christian worship, but she says, "Along with the rest of the Christian family I know myself to be very much a beginner in the process of learning how to worship." This book is thus a beginning for all beginners.

JOHN M. MULDER

Louisville Presbyterian Theological Seminary
Louisville, Kentucky

Part One

A THEOLOGY OF WORSHIP

1

THE PERIL OF WORSHIP

All human beings worship. At all times and in all places, in every known civilization, men and women have developed systems of symbolic language and ritual behavior to express their religious devotion. The very word "culture" comes from the Latin *cultus*, a synonym for worship. Our word "cultivate" comes from the same root. Caring and adoring are twin responses to what we think is most worthwhile.

Worship is a complex human activity. Sociologists and psychologists, archaeologists and cultural anthropologists, artists and poets can all teach us something about it. So can linguists and dramatists. No study of worship from one angle only can capture its many dimensions. Anyone who tries to reduce the rich symphony of worship to a single note is clearly tone-deaf.

Nevertheless this study of worship is written from the perspective of Christian theology. It asks you to think about worship from the angle of Christian faith. Therefore it begins by recognizing that worship is not always a good thing to do. In fact, worship can be dangerous.

The dangers of misdirected worship are forever etched in the memories of those of us who looked at pictures of corpses piled up at Jonestown a few years ago. The cultic frenzy which led to that appalling mass suicide of Americans living in Guyana is a complicated human story. It is not simply an instance of misdirected worship. Yet it is shocking evidence that any cultic activity, any human worship, has within it the potential for great evil.

The author of the last book in the Bible would agree. The Seer of the Apocalypse uses the verb "to worship" almost twice as many times as any other New Testament writer. In the Revised Standard Version, the word appears twenty-three times in Revelation and only nine times in the Gospel of Matthew, which is in second place on that score. But almost half of the times that worship is mentioned by name in Revelation, it is mentioned in a negative context. The great peril in the author's mind, one literally akin to suicide, was worship of the beast.

In the code language of the book of Revelation, written during active Roman persecution of Christians toward the end of the first century, "the beast" was the symbol for the emperor. Christians who refused to give divine worship to the emperor were executed. It was therefore a great temptation for Christians to worship "the beast," and so most of the Seer's denunciation of worshipers is against those who agreed to do so. But he also indicts those who worship demons and idols (Rev. 9:20), and he hears himself denounced for falling down to worship the angel who inspired his vision:

> You must not do that! I am a fellow servant with you and your brethren who hold the testimony of Jesus. Worship God. (Rev. 19:10)

According to this New Testament writer, worship is clearly not in itself a healthy human habit. Worship is judged by the object—or better, the subject—toward whom it is directed. That subject of true worship is God and God alone. If we are to explore the worship of God as Christians understand it, we need to focus both on the God whom we are worshiping and on the distinctive worship which *that* God inspires.

But we should not move too swiftly into a positive assessment of worship. The dangers of false worship are too many and too grave—as any reader of the Bible, of human history, and of the daily newspaper knows.

The book of Revelation highlights idolatry as a major danger. So does the rest of the Bible. The book of Revelation also identifies a second ever-present danger that lies in wait for worshipers—lukewarmness. The author does not seem particularly worried about a third ever-present danger in worship, that of getting carried away by fascination with the ritual words and actions for their own sake; but that danger was well known to other biblical writers. And such clutching of cherished words and actions as if they were in themselves a kind of security blanket seems to beset us still today. We need to look more closely at each of these three dangers before we turn to Christian worship in the light of the New Age. Since we still live partly in the Old Age, our worship is still perilous. It is still distorted by our bias on our own behalf.

Unfortunately "idolatry" has acquired an archaic sound in our ears. We think that it refers primarily to the worship of images carved of wood or stone. We assume that it refers to a literal worship of the golden calf that Aaron created out of the Israelites' jewelry, and thus we miss the psychological subtleties of the account of that crisis in Exodus 32. Or we conjure up mental pictures of Cromwell's soldiers smashing priceless statues in England's cathedrals and parish churches, with a fury inherited directly from Moses, and we distance ourselves from such fanaticism. If we look again, we can see more contemporary versions of idolatry all around us. Have we never watched a teenager wash a car? Or listened to people who really believe in the almighty dollar?

Idolatry as it is understood in the Bible and as it is practiced in our culture does not mean just a simpleminded belief that some ancient wood carving or some current product of Detroit or Tokyo assembly lines *is* itself ultimate reality. Rather, it means that giving our ultimate attention and devotion to anything finite and fabricated is, at best, stupid. At worst it is self-destructive.

No one to my knowledge has ever captured the basic life-or-death contrast between idolatry and true worship better than the poet called Second Isaiah. The gods of the Babylonians, he tells us with superb irony, have to be loaded onto wagons pulled by weary beasts, to be dragged through town in a festive processional on their annual excursion. They soon go back into captivity in the temple. Summing up the impotence of such an idol, he notes how the priests control it:

> They set it in its place, and it stands there;
> it cannot move from its place.
>
> (Isa. 46:7)

The Lord, the one true God, is different. He is not one who can be carried about. Instead, he is the one who has borne Israel from its birth, carried it from the womb. He does not just sit there. He moves under his own power.

Old Testament stories, often equally pointed and humorous, also sharpen the antithesis between the worship of God and the worship of substitutes. One example occurs in the cycle of legends about the prophet Elijah. The incident occurs on Mt. Carmel in the ninth century B.C. In it we are again confronted with a life-or-death contest between true worship and false worship.

Four hundred and fifty prophets of Baal are gathered to offer sacrifice to their god, according to *their* pattern of symbolic language and ritual action. One lone prophet of Yahweh, God of Israel, is prepared to do the same, according to *his* rites and ceremonies. Reread and enjoy the story in I Kings 18.

The priests of Baal limp about their outdoor altar in procession all morning long—and nothing happens. The prophet of Yahweh taunts them. Perhaps their god is off on a business trip, or taking a nap, or maybe he is just temporarily visiting the rest room. (Our translations are restrained about this suggestion.) Then the prophet of Yahweh comes center stage and we are treated to comic exaggeration. He douses the wood on the sacrificial fire not once but three times. And then he calls on, prays to, the Lord. Immediately the soaking-wet wood is ignited, and all the people fall on their faces (an action that means worship), saying, "The LORD, he is God; the LORD, he is God" (I Kings 18:39).

In both the Old Testament and the New, worship per se is not necessarily either praiseworthy or efficacious. The real question is, Who or what are you worshiping? The perils of wrongheaded worship are dramatized as vividly and as bloodily in the Elijah legend as in Revelation. At the end of the contest on Mt. Carmel, all of the four hundred and fifty prophets of Baal are promptly slaughtered.

Death by the sword evokes more colorful storytelling than death by ennui, yet that danger also snared worshipers in biblical times as well as in our own. The author of Revelation accuses the Christian church in Laodicea of being lukewarm in their works—including, by implication at least, their public work of worship, their liturgy (Rev. 2:16). The author of Hebrews also rebukes tepid worshipers who are neglecting to meet together (Heb. 10:25). He exhorts them to lift their drooping hands and strengthen their weak knees (Heb. 12:12).

Today our leaders of worship still call upon the Lord to deliver us from coldness of heart and wanderings of mind in worship. Lukewarmness also manifests itself in now-and-then churchgoing, and that sometimes out of a dull sense of duty. Lord Peter Wimsey, Dorothy L. Sayers' impeccable British detective, epitomizes that attitude when, in *Busman's Honeymoon,* he asks his new wife if she can possibly bear being hauled off to church. "I mean, it'll be kind of well-thought-of if we turn up in the family pew," he says; "gives people something to talk about and all that sort of thing."

The ho-hum quality of this offhand invitation to go to church on a Sunday morning is mildly amusing, a passing comment on the human comedy, until we remember that worship is a two-way relationship. Is it possible that God, too, gets bored with the kind of lukewarm worship we offer? That possibility—indeed, that probability—is inescapable if we listen to the prophet Malachi's denunciation of the Temple worship he knew in ancient Jerusalem. "You have wearied the LORD with your words," he says (Mal. 2:17).

Equally as dangerous as cooling off about worship, however, is getting overheated about it. The Bible recognizes the danger of overenthusiasm for worship as well as the pitfall of boredom with it. The mere noise of solemn assemblies exercises a certain fascination for some people; the rites of worship in themselves become all-absorbing. The prophet Amos saw such delight in externals of liturgy dominating Israel's worship, and he lashed out against it in the name of the Lord:

> "Come to Bethel, and transgress;
>   to Gilgal, and multiply transgression;
> bring your sacrifices every morning,
>   your tithes every three days; . . .
>   for so you love to do, O people of Israel!"
>   says the Lord GOD.
>
> (Amos 4:4–5)

Through Amos, the Lord rejects the offerings of fatted beasts and well-tuned harps. He demands offerings of justice and righteousness instead.

In a somewhat different form, overenthusiasm about worship shows up hundreds of years later in the Christian church at Corinth. It evokes one of the apostle Paul's most important discussions of the early Eucharist and of the role of the Holy Spirit in worship. We will return to his positive thought on the subject. For the moment it is important to notice that Paul, like Amos, realized how easy it is to get carried away in worship and thus to forget the needs of others, especially of hungry people and outsiders.

The criticisms that Amos and Paul levy against the human capacity for twisting worship out of shape, for moving it off target, have notable differences. Amos seems to be charging Israel with formalism, with overfixation on external rituals. Paul seems to be charging the New Israel with informality, with a failure to do things decently and in order. But they share a common conviction that worship is fundamentally connected with the rest of life, and that if worship activities are heated to a fever pitch, such interconnections tend to be lost from sight.

An underlying similarity between the poles of form and freedom in worship—or, at the extremes, between formalism and formlessness—will also demand further attention. Both seem to result, however, from overfixation on worship understood as a human enterprise carried on and carried out as if it were its own raison d'être—as if it were simply an aesthetic art form on the one hand, or an orgy of human emotion on the other. Contemporary caricatures of the denunciations of worship brought by Amos and Paul respectively might depict, perhaps, an Anglican cathedral choir "doing" a Bach B Minor Mass versus a television evangelist inducing unleashed enthusiasm in the audience. Although the sawdust trail may now be covered with red carpet on our television screens, the threat of a spiritual elitism such as Paul sensed in the Corinthian situation has not lessened in the Christian church.

Over against these dangers of idolatry, lukewarmness, and overheating, the Bible proposes to us a cardinal text for thinking about Christian worship. It comes from John's

Gospel. It announces *the* difference between true worship
and false worship, *the* difference between true worship
and the twisted and distorted forms of this cherished and
universal human activity. The authentic article is identified very simply:

> God is spirit, and those who worship him must worship in
> spirit and truth. (John 4:24)

Accordingly we will turn now to the role of God the
Holy Spirit in Christian worship, to the ways in which God
the Spirit is the one who makes it possible truly to enter
his courts with praise. As we noted at the beginning of this
chapter, if we are to grow in the understanding of worship
as Christians try to practice it, we must constantly remember the One we are worshiping. Since Christians believe
in a triune God—one spoken of as God the Father, God the
Son, and God the Holy Spirit—a trinitarian structure will
shape the theology of worship in the chapters that follow.

If we are to guard against the dangers we have identified in this chapter, especially the danger of idolatry, we
will have to face on the way the limitations of our inherited language for speaking to God and about God. At this
juncture we bow not only to Scripture but also to tradition,
and hence to the words of the so-called Athanasian Creed.
It is one of our inherited definitions of who it is that Christians believe to be the focus of their worship: "We worship
one God in Trinity, and Trinity in Unity, neither con-
founding the Persons, nor dividing the Substance." In the
worship of that one God, the Holy Spirit plays a decisive
role, but so also do the Son and the Father. As we divide
the Persons for purposes of deepening our understanding
of worship, we will try to remain unitarian about God's
substance. The imperative from Revelation is clear: "Worship God!"

2

THE ACTION
OF THE SPIRIT

"God is spirit," John tells us, "and those who worship him must worship in spirit and truth." That sentence from the Fourth Gospel says that true Christian worship is a matter of right relations between human spirits and God's Spirit. As we begin to think about the action of God the Spirit in initiating and sustaining lively worship in the Christian community, we need to emphasize that element of dynamic, personal relationship.

Many of the metaphors that the Bible uses to talk about the activity of God in worship make the Holy Spirit sound like an impersonal force or energy—something like an electric current or a volatile liquid with radioactive properties. When we talk about God's instigation of authentic worship, however, we need to insist that only personal pronouns are adequate. God is never an it.

Nor is God the Holy Spirit to be thought of just as a vague oblong blur, which is the best image some of us can come up with. Mentally handicapped by the archaic language, "Holy Ghost," many of us grew up with an unconscious picture of the Spirit not very much different from the sheet-draped spook on a Halloween greeting card. We did not learn that in the person of the Holy Spirit we have to do with the God who comes to be among us—with the One whom John V. Taylor, Bishop of Winchester, has aptly named "the Go-Between God."

This Go-Between God gives us the gift that enables us to worship. This Go-Between God empowers us to worship in such a way that our lives are changed, and so also the world around us. This Go-Between God creates a community, a commonwealth of worship which unites us one to the other so that no one ever prays alone. In thinking about worship as gift and as power and as commonweal, we need to keep reminding ourselves that worship always takes place on at least a two-lane highway.

One of the best-known medieval hymns still in regular use in Christian worship bears the Latin title "Veni, Creator Spiritus." No one knows who actually wrote it, but tradition links it with a ninth-century archbishop of Mainz, Rabanus Maurus, who also wrote one of the earliest-known essays on the theology of the Lord's Supper. Scholars tell us that none of the many English translations of the hymn captures the power of the Latin original. Among them are: "Come, Holy Ghost, Creator blest . . ."; "O come, Creator Spirit, come. . . ." In 1693 the English poet John Dryden tried his hand at it. In his version the first line reads, "Creator Spirit, by whose aid . . ." The invocations continue: "come, visit," "come, pour." The first stanza ends, "And make thy temples worthy thee."

Since at least 856, then, Christian worshipers have used such words to invite God the Holy Spirit to be present among them as they worship. They have recognized that only God can and does make temples or churches or any other assembly place of Christian people worthy of bearing his name. Recalling that the word "worship" at its root means giving worth to, we acknowledge that we can give worth to God only because God first gives worth to us. This assertion lies close to the heart of Christian worship, even as it lies close to the mystery of all of God's relationships with us.

Our basic capacity truly to worship is the result of a prior gift of the creative Spirit of God. God instigates the whole business. God also sustains it. The hymn "Veni, Creator Spiritus" proceeds to speak of the Spirit's "sevenfold gifts of grace," or, in another translation, "the sevenfold gift of grace." Whether in the singular or the plural, the allusion goes back to a list of spiritual gifts cited by the prophet Isaiah in the Greek version of a song that was probably written for the coronation of a king of Israel (Isa. 11:2). If one follows the Hebrew text, one finds that only six gifts are enumerated. In Christian usage, however, those royal virtues such as wisdom and understanding and counsel and might came to be associated with prayer for persons being confirmed in the church and with prayer for persons being ordained for leadership in its ministry.

The difference between six gifts of the Spirit in the Hebrew text and seven in the Greek is not reported merely as a bit of academic trivia. Rather it is, I think, a prophetic warning. Christians have quibbled about gifts of the Spirit from the fifties of the first century until the present day. In the fifties in Corinth the quarrel was over which gifts of the Spirit each worshiper had and whose gift was the best. The quarrel among Christians today is not far different. Must one speak in tongues in order to worship God most fully? Or is the gift of prophecy necessary? Are there six or seven gifts, thirteen or thirty? Or perhaps only one?

When Paul wrote to the Christians at Corinth about these questions, he was inspired by the Holy Spirit to speak of love. The great hymn about Christian agape, about God's love, which we know as I Corinthians 13, is Paul's definitive answer to any argument about spiritual gifts. The greatest of them is love. Paul's verdict in that letter parallels his ringing assertion about God's great gift, which comes to us in his letter to the church at Rome: "God's love has been poured into our hearts through the Holy Spirit which has been given to us" (Rom. 5:5).

Christian worship acts out a love relation. And that relation is initiated by a Christmas present which is also an Easter present and a Pentecost present. The three most important celebrations of the Christian year, the three greatest festivals of Christian worship, rejoice annually in the one fact of amazing grace. The God whom Christians worship comes to us in love, seeks us out, draws us into his presence. The human capacity for worship that is truly alive is an unsolicited donation from the Author of Life.

Not only does the Go-Between God send us that gift of love which ignites worship. God the Spirit is also the one who makes worship an activity of enormous power. The New Testament tells us that we should expect any experience of God's Spirit to be filled with power. The Greek word translated "power" is in fact *dynamis,* from which we get our English word "dynamite."

At the end of Luke's Gospel, Jesus charges his disciples to stay in Jerusalem until they are "clothed with power from on high" (Luke 24:49). At the beginning of Luke's second volume, The Acts of the Apostles, the risen Lord again promises the disciples that they "shall receive power" when the Holy Spirit comes upon them (Acts 1:8). After that Pentecost event the apostles exhibit extraordinary powers, as the rest of the book of Acts testifies. Not the least of these powers was that of steadfast devotion to "the breaking of bread and the prayers" (Acts 2:42).

Paul similarly stressed the fact that the Holy Spirit is the one who empowers believers. By the power of the Holy Spirit Christians "abound in hope" (Rom. 15:13); through the power of the Holy Spirit, Paul himself is the agent of "signs and wonders" (Rom. 15:19). He preached the gospel "in demonstration of the Spirit and of power" (I Cor. 2:4). His gospel came to the infant churches in Greece not only in word "but also in power and in the Holy Spirit" (I Thess. 1:5).

What is the meaning of such scriptural reports of power?

And how are we to interpret them today? How do they relate to our worship on an ordinary Sunday morning?

The account of the Day of Pentecost when the gift of the Holy Spirit was given to the early disciples notes that "they were all together in one place" (Acts 2:1). It is probable that they had come together for worship. Two major images are then used to describe what happened. They *heard* a sound "like the rush of a mighty wind." They *saw* what appeared to them to be tongues of fire.

Both wind and fire continue to be classic symbols for the Holy Spirit at work in the world. Each of them is a natural symbol, expressing at least two dimensions of human experience. Wind may come to us as a gentle breeze in the cool of the evening, or it may blow with hurricane force. Fire may crackle merrily in the grate, a cozy blaze to warm us on a cold winter's night; or it may rage out of control in the dry grass and destroy dozens of southern California homes. Precisely because they are ambiguous, wind and fire are superb symbols for the Holy. The Holy at once fascinates us with its magnetic attraction and, at the same time, warns us to stand back in awe.

In the history of Christian worship most of the church has emphasized the gentler side of its symbols for the work of the Spirit of God in its midst. It has been understandably wary of their dimensions of force and great power. The idea of special power imparted by the Spirit in the context of worship has, indeed, often been linked with either heretical or sectarian movements on the fringes of the church.

In the second century, for example, Montanus, an enthusiastic revivalist, spoke to his followers of the power given them. His companion, Maximilla, in a moment of prophecy, spoke of herself as "word, spirit, and power." An anonymous critic of that time charged that in worship Montanus fell into abnormal ecstasy "to such an extent that he became frenzied and began to babble." As for

Maximilla, the critic believed that it was not the Holy Spirit who spoke through her, but a spurious spirit, a talkative spirit, a maddening spirit. The church historian Eusebius called it simply a bastard spirit. The Montanists were judged to be heretics.

In the sixteenth century, to cite another example, the "left wing" of the Reformation was similarly criticized by the dominant church for effervescence in worship. The founders of what came to be known as the "free churches" stressed a freedom in worship comparable to the freedom they believed existed in New Testament times. Partly in reaction against their views on worship, Luther said that they appeared to have swallowed the Holy Spirit "feathers and all."

The Lutherans had a general term of abuse for such spiritualists—*Schwärmerei.* An English descendant of the "spiritual Reformers," J. S. Whale, once explained the meaning of the term as "what would happen if we brushed our teeth with shaving soap." It really means "foaming at the mouth," he said. The terms "Quakers" and "Shakers" were also invented originally to ridicule Christian behavior in worship which gave expression to the powerful presence of the Spirit.

In our own day a resurgent sense of the Spirit's powerful action in Christian worship is evident not only among those whom we call Pentecostals but also among many Protestants and Roman Catholics who have been dubbed Neo-Pentecostals or Charismatics. Like the Montanists and the Anabaptists before them, they also have evoked suspicions of heresy and separatism.

Nevertheless the experience of power in worship to which this "third world" of Christendom testifies demands our respectful attention. One vivid firsthand account of such an experience, which took place in 1960, translates the Pentecostal fire imagery straight from the New Testament into twentieth-century idiom:

It was like a thousand—like ten thousand—then a million
volts of electricity. . . . I could hear, as it were, a zooming
sound of power. It pulled my hands higher and held them
there as though God took them in His.

The Christian pastor writing this account continues with
more metaphors of fire. In an air-conditioned room he felt
"the hot, molten lava" of God's love. His body perspired
as though he was "in a steam bath." And because he was
thereafter empowered to share his new relationship with
God, the account concludes, other men and women who
formerly "trudged wearily to prayer meeting" became
instead "flaming evangels for Jesus."

Such language encounters earmuffs on many Christians
accustomed to living in colder climates. The heirs of the
Calvinist or Lutheran or Anglican traditions of the Reformation are often uncomfortable in the presence of "en-
thusiasts." So are most heirs of Trent and the Counter-
Reformation in Roman Catholicism. In this metaphoric
context, we may rightly be labeled God's frozen people.
We sometimes stiffen up even at John Wesley's claim that
his heart was "strangely warmed" at Aldersgate.

When we attend to the role of God the Holy Spirit in
worship, in the New Testament and throughout Christian
history, however, we find ourselves continually challenged by fire. And, as J. S. Whale also remarked, "without
this fire, religion is dead ashes."

So far in this chapter we have said that the gift of the
Spirit enables us to worship and that the power of the
Spirit enlivens us through worship. God the Spirit also
creates community through worship. The Spirit is that
persona of the triune Being whose role is unitive. The
Spirit is the one who unites us to God and to each other.
In all reverence, the Go-Between God might even be
called God the glue.

Spatial language always poses dangers for our thinking
about God. God is as much down under as up there.

Nevertheless, the vocabulary of height is embedded in Christian tradition, and we can learn through it about our love relation with God as it is expressed and evoked in Christian worship. So also God is as much in my inmost self as out there in my sister or my brother. Nevertheless the vocabulary of breadth is equally a part of our heritage, and it continues to teach us about reaching out. The vertical and the horizontal relations of worship will be constant themes throughout this study. Both are essential because Christian worship must be cruciform. While we are still focused on God the Spirit, however, both dimensions of the Spirit's work need to be underlined.

The vertical work of the Spirit is well captured by Ignatius of Antioch in his letter to the church at Ephesus, a letter written in the early years of the second century. He pictures you and me as so many cement blocks being hoisted up, yet at the same time as so many mountain climbers climbing up. That passive-active dialectic is striking when he asks us to think of the Holy Spirit as a rope:

> Like stones of God's Temple, ready for a building of God the Father, you are being hoisted up by Jesus Christ as with a crane (that's the cross!), while the rope you use is the Holy Spirit. (Ad Eph. 9:1)

Alongside this picture of the way in which our hearts are lifted to God in worship, there belongs another image from our tradition. In this sixteenth-century prayer, we are asked to think of the Holy Spirit not as a rope but as yarn:

> Almighty God, who hast knit together thine elect in one communion and fellowship . . .

In the background of that venerable prayer for All Saints' Day lie the closing words of Paul in what we call his Second Letter to the Corinthians, when he speaks of "the fellowship of the Holy Spirit." In the foreground is the intricate interconnection of the yarn in the sleeve of your sweater. God the Holy Spirit who hoists us up in worship is also the Spirit who unites us one to the other as tenaciously and as tenderly as the knit-one, purl-one pattern of a Shetland cardigan.

3
THE ROLE OF JESUS
THE CHRIST

Christian worship is rooted in Judaism. Jesus was a Jew. The earliest Christians also were Jews. Their patterns of worship were deeply influenced by the worship of the synagogue, and therefore our patterns of worship today still bear the marks of their birthplace. The Temple in Jerusalem is mentioned so frequently in the New Testament that we sometimes overlook the importance of synagogues.

Sunday school pictures of Jesus and illustrations in many Bibles almost always show Jesus teaching out of doors. We come to think of him sitting in a boat, speaking to crowds gathered on the sunlit shore, or standing on a grassy hillside surrounded by throngs of common people listening to his parables. Yet all four Gospels make the synagogue a focal place for Jesus' teaching, and one Gospel says that he went to the synagogue on the Sabbath Day "as his custom was" (Luke 4:16). Jesus evidently practiced corporate worship.

Mark begins his portrait of Jesus' public ministry in the synagogue at Capernaum. "Immediately on the sabbath he entered the synagogue and taught" (Mark 1:21). He also healed a man there. Mark adds later that Jesus went throughout all Galilee, "preaching in their synagogues and casting out demons" (Mark 1:39).

Visitors to Capernaum today can see the ruins of the synagogue there, near the palm-lined shores of the Sea of Galilee. Built of gleaming white limestone, the synagogue was adorned with twenty-foot columns topped by Corinthian capitals. Six of them have been reconstructed so that the visitor can get some idea of the height of the building. The main room for worship was in the shape of a rectangle with some sixty by eighty feet of floor space.

Archaeologists conclude that these ruins date from the second century, and therefore it is not the same building that Jesus preached in, not the one the centurion helped to finance, according to Luke 7:5. Nevertheless it stands on the site of an older synagogue, and it reminds us of the physical prominence of synagogue buildings in the towns and villages of Palestine even in the first century—buildings extremely influential in the lives of the people.

Luke, on the other hand, begins his portrait of Jesus' public ministry not in Capernaum but in the synagogue at Nazareth. He gives us a glimpse of what the service was like. His brief account accords with what we know about ancient synagogue worship from other sources.

An opening recitation of the Shema announced: "Hear, O Israel: The LORD our God is one LORD; and you shall love the LORD your God with all your heart, and with all your soul, and with all your might" (Deut. 6:4–5). Some prayers and an appointed reading from the Torah followed. It was read in Hebrew but was immediately translated into the local vernacular—Aramaic in Nazareth in Jesus' day. A second reading was freely chosen from the scrolls of the prophets. The elders of the synagogue customarily invited anyone in the congregation to share in leadership at this point. Judaism then as now was a lay religion. Although he stood to read, the lector sat down to comment on the Scripture passage. The service closed with a benediction, often the familiar one from Num. 6: 24–26: "The LORD bless you and keep you: The LORD

make his face to shine upon you, and be gracious to you:
The LORD lift up his countenance upon you, and give you
peace."

Jesus' sermon at Nazareth becomes for Luke a program-
matic introduction to the major themes of his version of
the gospel. The reading that Jesus chose from the scroll of
the prophet Isaiah announces what he will thereafter say
and do—preach good news to the poor and set at liberty
those who are oppressed. We do not have the transcript of
the sermon he preached with the eyes of everyone in the
synagogue fixed upon him. We know only that he began
by saying, "Today this scripture has been fulfilled in your
hearing" (Luke 4:21). But Luke, at least, is certain that this
sermon was "in the power of the Spirit" (Luke 4:14).

All the Gospels emphasize Jesus' regular presence at
worship in particular places at particular times. All four
Gospels also stress Jesus' practice of private prayer. They
all give us a clear picture of a man who habitually went off
by himself, or in the company of some close friends, to
pray for refreshment in times of fatigue, for guidance in
times of decision, for support in times of crisis. The historical Jesus as we meet him in the New Testament lived a life
of prayer in close personal communion with God.

Out of his own experience of prayer and worship, therefore, Jesus was able to respond to his friends when they
asked him, "Lord, teach us to pray" (Luke 11:1). His clear-
est answer to that request begins, "When you pray, say:
'Father, hallowed be thy name . . .' " The prayer has come
down to us in two slightly different versions. The one in
Luke's Gospel (Luke 11:2–4) is shorter and more primitive
in form; that in Matt. 6:9–13 is more developed, showing
the effects of repeated use in Christian worship before it
was written down to be included as part of the Sermon on
the Mount.

The impact of the Lord's Prayer on subsequent Christian worship is incalculable. It has played a decisive part

in Christian reflection on the meaning of prayer and worship as well. In the early church, catechumens, those in training to become full-fledged Christians, learned it by rote as part of the *traditio* handed over to them before baptism. They were charged to pray it three times daily. One twentieth-century Christian, a saintly man of God nearing the end of his life, clearly understood the enormity of that charge. When asked what he hoped to accomplish in his remaining years, it is reported, he replied simply, "To pray one good 'Our Father' before I die."

The oldest-known discussions of the nature of Christian prayer all use "The Prayer" for a springboard. A treatise on prayer by Origen, which has been called the oldest extant "scientific discussion" of Christian prayer, depends on it. Tertullian and Cyprian in the West, Gregory of Nyssa and Theodore of Mopsuestia in the East, among others, have left us tracts or catechetical homilies on the subject. Their commentaries direct our attention especially to the invocation and to three major petitions of the prayer. They underline Jesus' own teaching on prayer as the New Testament presents it to us.

First, "Our Father." We will have more to say about this opening phrase in the next chapter. The fathers of the church also had much to say about it, but their major emphasis was on the priorities of prayer which the phrase indicates. Prayer starts with God and moves to us.

Second, "Thy kingdom come." Here greater differences existed between Eastern and Western understanding of the petition. Nevertheless one finds a profound and ecumenical agreement that the Kingdom of God, or the sovereignty of God, was central to Jesus' understanding of reality. God reigns, and realization of that fact is about to dawn like thunder among us.

The other two petitions in the pattern prayer to which our early theologians paid most attention were "Thy will be done" and "Give us this day our daily bread." The former incited sober enthusiasm for prayer as an avenue for conforming our wills, our aspirations, our desires to those of God. Every reader of the New Testament is driven to the Garden of Gethsemane, where the historical Jesus wrestled one black night with his human desire to escape execution. His recorded prayer is all that needs to be said to interpret what we mean when we say, "Thy will be done."

In the petition asking for our daily bread, however, patristic exegetes found three dimensions. They elaborated on our total dependence on God, on our need to limit our desires to the basic necessities of life, and—as their most distinctively Christian contribution to the subject of worship—on our participation in the Eucharist, hailed as *the* daily bread of life.

At this point in their commentaries on the Lord's Prayer, Tertullian, Gregory, and the rest put before us the other decisive aspect of Jesus' teaching about prayer and worship—as incalculable in its influence as is the pattern prayer Jesus taught us. Not only did he tell us to *say,* "Our Father . . .," he also told us to *do* something. On the night he was arrested, he gathered his friends around him at supper. And he took bread, blessed it, broke it, and gave it to them. And he said, "Do this in remembrance of me."

Jesus of Nazareth, then, Jesus the first-century Palestinian Jew, left us an inheritance of example and command. His example both calls us together for worship and sends us apart for the same purpose. His command directs us to say certain words and to do certain things. He is the rabbi who teaches us what it means to worship God in spirit and in truth.

As our crucified and risen Lord, however, Jesus the Christ plays a continuing role in Christian worship, a role anchored not in the synagogues of Galilee but in the courts of heaven. The New Testament has two chief ways of talking about this present action of the incarnate Lord, action that grounds our worship in today's reality. It declares that he lives to intercede for us. It reminds us that we worship "in his name."

In the person of the risen Lord we have a friend at court. The author of Hebrews "discourses at length" on this subject, as John Calvin puts it, "from the seventh almost to the end of the tenth chapter." The discourse concerns Jesus as our High Priest who has entered once for all into the Holy of Holies. Unlike the human high priests of Judaism, who had to be replaced whenever they died, Jesus Christ holds his priesthood permanently. "Consequently he is able for all time to save those who draw near to God through him, since he always lives to make intercession for them" (Heb. 7:25). Drawing near to God, in the idiom of Hebrews, means worshiping.

Unlike the old sanctuary built by human hands, furthermore, the place that Christ has entered is heaven itself, "now to appear in the presence of God on our behalf" (Heb. 9:24). The author of Hebrews believes that this past and present work of Christ has consequences for worship. Since Christ has opened for us a "new and living way" to God, therefore we can "draw near with a true heart in full assurance of faith" (Heb. 10:20, 22).

When he explains these difficult ideas from Hebrews, as part of his discussion of Christ's office as priest, Calvin reminds us that the term "Christ," or "Messiah," means "the anointed one." Under the old law of Judaism, priests as well as kings and prophets were anointed with holy oil when they were instituted in their new office. Such oil was also called "unction," a word that comes from the Latin word for "anointing." In Calvin's mind, since Christ is head of the church, "from him as head this unction is diffused through the members." We are not ourselves worthy to storm up to the throne of God under our own steam. But since Christ now bears the office of priest, he is allied with God. And, Calvin concludes in a tone of awe, he admits us "into this most honorable alliance." In him we can "offer ourselves and our all to God, and freely enter the heavenly sanctuary" (Calvin, *Institutes of the Christian Religion,* II. xv. 6).

Although only Hebrews elaborates the metaphor of Christ's high priesthood in the New Testament, Paul also describes Christ as the one who stands beside God and stands there as our ally and friend. The identification comes in the midst of a passage of ringing rhetoric, beginning, "If God is for us, who is against us?" The passage ends with the passionate assertion that nothing can ever "separate us from the love of God in Christ Jesus our Lord" (Rom. 8:31–39). In this context Christ Jesus is described as the one who died, who was raised, who is at the right hand of God, and who "indeed intercedes for us."

Calvin cites this sentence from Romans when he is explaining what the Apostles' Creed means when it says that Christ is seated at the right hand of God. He is convinced that that Creed was "certainly written for popular use," even though we do not know who actually wrote it. He is also convinced that the term "seated" does not refer primarily to the position of Christ's body, so we need not get upset when someone reports a vision of Christ standing. Rather, Calvin argues, the phrase means that Christ is presiding. It means that everything is placed at his disposal. It means also that "we are in a manner now seated in heavenly places, not entertaining a mere hope of heaven, but possessing it in our head" (Calvin, *Institutes of the Christian Religion,* II. xvi. 16). He means, of course, in Christ our Head.

Mythological language about thrones in heaven and anthropomorphic metaphors about sitting at God's right hand present difficulties for our religious imaginations today; but the power of a name is fully recognized in our culture. Computers print our names in capital letters on the front of unsolicited catalogs, urging us to enter the sweepstakes, take advantage of the sale, order our spring bulbs now. We know the feeling that people are trying to manipulate us through the use of our names, and so we can sense something of the magic powers, even the dark powers, associated with names in the minds of our ancestors. The extreme care the Israelites took to avoid using the name of Yahweh lightly is one example of this ancient attitude toward naming.

Against this background, the climax of the early Christological hymn in Paul's letter to the church at Philippi has added power: "At the name of Jesus every knee should bow, in heaven and on earth and under the earth, and every tongue confess that Jesus Christ is Lord, to the glory of God the Father" (Phil. 2:10–11). Again we are in a context of worship. The hymn as a whole tells us why Christians have for centuries routinely ended their prayers with the formula, ". . . through Jesus Christ our Lord. Amen."

We worship in the name of Jesus Christ because God united himself to human being in that one person. Human beings are irrevocably united with God, bonded to him, through the person of Christ. We bear his name and he bears ours. He wears our nature and invites us to come into communion with his. Christian worship occurs because of that awesome connection between humanity and deity—effected in the event of Jesus the Christ, through his life and his death and his resurrection. So we worship in the power of his Spirit. We worship in his name. And we worship in thanksgiving for his great gift of new relationship.

4

MAKER OF HEAVEN AND EARTH

Jesus the Christ invites us into new relationship with God in and through our worship. He teaches us that we can have an extraordinarily intimate relationship with God the Father, although our first reaction to God's holy presence may be to take off our shoes or to fall flat on our faces. He shows us that God stretches our ways of thinking about and of speaking to him. And he makes it clear that the heavenly Father whom we worship is the one who clothes the lilies and feeds the birds of the sky. Indeed God is the maker of all that is.

One word evokes the extraordinary intimacy of Christian worship—the Aramaic word *abba*. It is a term borrowed from the vocabulary of children. Some commentators say that it approximates our American term "daddy." That is not altogether a happy comparison, since it is hard to think of the almighty Creator in any way analogous to that in which we think about the human daddy who pays the check for hamburgers. "Daddy" sounds disrespectful to us, overly casual for our approach to the ruler of the universe. But for that very reason it tells us a lot about the quality of tenderness with which Jesus spoke to God. In Jesus' mind, God was very near and very close. We can properly approach him in childlike trust.

Early Christians continued to use that Aramaic word to

address God, even in Asia Minor and Rome. Paul uses "Abba" in two of his letters written to Greek-speaking congregations about the middle of the first century. He tells the Galatian Christians that they are no longer slaves, but full members of the family of God. Because God has sent the Spirit of his Son into their hearts, they are enabled and entitled to cry, "Abba! Father!" (Gal. 4:6). Again, he reminds the Roman Christians that when they cry, "Abba! Father!" they show that they are led by the Spirit into full and fearless stature as heirs along with Christ (Rom. 8:15).

Almost certainly Paul can make these references to the term "Abba" with evident expectation that everyone will know what he is talking about, because the Christians to whom he is writing in ancient Turkey and Italy already used that same word in their worship—a word inherited from Jesus' own language and teaching. The word was almost certainly passed on by the first disciples as they taught others what Jesus had taught them about praying.

The term "Abba" occurs in the New Testament a third time. That occurrence calls for special attention because Jesus himself uses it in his prayer in the Garden of Gethsemane as recorded in Mark's Gospel. There, on the night before he was crucified, Jesus prays that, if possible, he might be saved from impending torture and death. According to Mark, he said, "Abba, Father, all things are possible to thee; remove this cup from me; yet not what I will, but what thou wilt" (Mark 14:36).

Mark's Gospel does not otherwise record Jesus' teaching about prayer, at which we looked earlier. It contains no complete text of the Our Father such as we found in Matthew and Luke. Not surprisingly, some scholars have therefore described this prayer of Jesus, which was prayed in the critical hours before his execution, as Mark's version of the Lord's Prayer. They mean by this that Mark and the Christian community to which he was writing clearly knew and used a common prayer taught them by those

who had known Jesus—the prayer that began in his native
tongue, "Abba!" It was a prayer they had learned to recite
bilingually, as it were. When they cried "Abba!" they immediately translated that word into their own language:
"Abba! Father!"

Very few of us know any Greek, much less Aramaic. Our
culture inevitably teaches us a notion of fatherhood different from that of the first century in Palestine or in Turkey
or in Rome. Fathers have their day on our calendar each
June. Fathers may still evoke more automatic respect than
do mothers, although that is questionable in our changing
times. Do we understand by our English and American
word "Father" anything at all like Jesus meant by "Abba"?

We don't know. There are no definitive answers to that
question. But we do know that when Jesus said "Abba" he
was not addressing either a remote sky god or an austere
and judgmental tribal patriarch. He was speaking with
someone he knew well and knew to be trustworthy, one
he could approach trustingly. And the marvel is that he
invited you and me to share in his approach, so that we too,
as the ancient liturgical formula puts it, can be "bold to
say, Our Father . . ."

The preservation of the term "Abba" in Christian liturgy offers us, I think, a master key for opening the win-
dows of our minds and hearts. When we call God "Father," we are not meant to think of a male deity. We are
meant to realize that God transcends "body, parts, or pas-
sions," as the Reformers insisted. We are also meant to
encounter "the ground of our being."

Paul Tillich, one of the greatest theologians of the twen-
tieth century, wrote prophetically on this subject back in
1963. He thought that his term for God, "ground of
being," transcended the masculine-feminine dichotomy
in our thinking about God and, indeed, fostered our recognition of the feminine dimensions in deity. Almost twenty
years ago, when commenting on trinitarian symbolism, he

said that the term "ground of being" points to "the mother-quality of giving birth, carrying, and embracing." Even then he was concerned to reduce the prominence of male imagery in thinking about God. He found feminine elements in the Logos and the Spirit as well (Tillich, *Systematic Theology*, Vol. III, p. 294).

The masculine associations of the image of God the Father have not dominated either Scripture or tradition as thoroughly as many critics would lead us to believe. In our day scholars have admittedly scoured the sources to counteract that charge. As a result they have repolished both Scripture and tradition to our great benefit.

The Old Testament scholar Phyllis Trible, for example, has demonstrated beyond a shadow of a doubt that in biblical metaphor Yahweh had a womb. Yahweh, the God of Israel, brought Israel to birth. Yahweh nourished, cherished, carried Israel. God stooped down to tend to the infant nation's needs.

Other recent efforts to rediscover the feminine in our common heritage have celebrated the mystic visions of Lady Julian of Norwich, the medieval British Christian of great sanctity who spoke often of Christ as our mother. Less often cited from the tradition to support the idea of "Abba! Father!" as a nonmasculine figure is the great seventeenth-century Anglican poet and preacher John Donne.

In one of his sermons, Donne wrestles with a fascinating passage from Numbers 11, in which a rebellious Moses protests to the Lord that he, Moses, did not conceive the people Israel, so he finds it unreasonable to be asked to carry them in his bosom "as a nurse carries the sucking child" (Num. 11:12). As far as Donne knew Scripture, "there and only there doth *Moses* attribute even to God himself the feminine sex." His conclusion from this passage stretches our understanding of God the Father, the God who is love, in the same way that Jesus had stretched it by calling God "Abba." Reacting to Moses and meditating on Numbers, John Donne said, "All that is good then, either in the love of man or woman is in this love, for he is expressed in both sexes, man and woman."

God the Father, therefore, according to Scripture and tradition, is not a macho figure. God is one we can appropriately think of as including both masculine and feminine traits. The confession of faith in God the Father Almighty asks us to trust in him also as maker of heaven and earth. According to the newest agreed-upon translation of the ancient text of the Nicene Creed, that means creator "of all that is, seen and unseen." This declaration of faith adds three new dimensions to our theology of worship.

First, the whole created world has a rightful role in worship. Israel's poets, in fact, picture all of nature responding in joy to the coming of the Lord. The psalmist, for example, asks all the earth to break forth in song:

> Let the sea roar, and all that fills it;
>   the world and those who dwell in it!
> Let the floods clap their hands;
>   let the hills sing for joy together.
>   (Ps. 98:7–8)

Similarly, Second Isaiah foresees a time of renewal when the mountains and hills shall break into song, and the trees of the field shall clap their hands (Isa. 55:12). Such images invite us to see our worship as part of the response which the whole created order makes to its Creator.

Thankful response for and with the gifts of creation has always been a part of Jewish and Christian worship. Cakes of fine flour mixed with oil and baked on a griddle, baskets of fruit, sheaves of grain—the directions for worship in the first five books of the Bible, Israel's Torah, describe such offerings in loving detail. The early Christians brought olives and cheese and oil to offer in worship, as well as bread and wine. Agricultural festivals gave way to historical festivals in the development of our tradition, as we shall see, but our worship has never lost its connections with seedtime and harvest. It has always affirmed the goodness of the material world.

Second, worship of God, who made the world and saw that it was very good, is embodied worship. You and I engage in intimate relation with our Creator as psychosomatic selves, incarnate selves. We are an inextricable fusion of flesh and spirit. This basic fact of human existence has often been viewed as unfortunate, and sometimes denied altogether. People have thought that they could worship as if they were disembodied spirits. They have thought that they could worship better if they either ignored their bodies entirely or pummeled them into submission through harsh ascetic practices.

The Christian affirmation of God's good creation, on the contrary, means that we are meant to worship with our whole selves, including all our senses. Our eyes and our ears, our hands and our feet, even our noses, are rightly participant. Our outward activity and our inward activity cannot be separated. Their intimate interconnection is beautifully expressed in a metaphor from an ancient song of penitence, "And now, O Lord, I bend the knee of my heart." Paul spoke of the same human wholeness when he exhorted us: "Present your bodies as a living sacrifice, holy and acceptable to God, which is your spiritual worship" (Rom. 12:1).

A third consequence of the doctrine of creation for a theology of worship is suggested by the statement that God the Father is the author of everything that is, "seen and unseen." When we worship together as a community of living Christians, we do not worship alone. We worship "with all the company of heaven." We worship also as part of "the communion of saints."

Both of these ideas are expressed in some of the oldest liturgies of the church. They are ideas rooted in Scripture.

But they were the subject of much heated debate at the time of the Reformation, and they pose enormous intellectual problems for the contemporary believer, infected as most of us are by rationalist presuppositions.

The former phrase, "with all the company of heaven," comes from the ancient preface to the song "Holy, Holy, Holy" used for centuries in Christian worship: "Therefore we praise you, joining our voices with angels and archangels, and with all the company of heaven, who for ever sing this hymn to proclaim the glory of your Name." We are reminded of the seraphim singing "Holy, holy, holy" in Isaiah's vision in the Temple in Jerusalem (Isa. 6:3). We are reminded of the four "living creatures" repeating the same song round the throne of God in Rev. 4:9.

The latter phrase, "the communion of saints," found its way into the Apostles' Creed about the end of the fourth century. At that time Bishop Niceta of Remesiana interpreted it to mean the union in the holy, catholic church of the whole company of heaven together with all who were, or are, or will be justified. Some scholars think that the same Niceta wrote the timeless hymn of praise, Te Deum Laudamus, "We praise you, O God . . ."

The Reformers were not happy with what they called "popish" ideas of invocation of the saints and prayers for the dead. They were uneasy about talk of communion in worship with "the church triumphant." They much preferred to limit intercessions to members of "the church militant here in earth." This shrinking of the received tradition probably helped promote a corresponding growth of human pretensions. By the end of the eighteenth century we no longer thought of ourselves as about at the midpoint of a great chain of being, with angels and archangels and other invisible creatures above us. Rather, we thought of ourselves as the highest of God's creatures. We were left only with what Peter Berger has aptly called "a rumor of angels."

Impossible as it may be for many of us today to repopulate the universe with angels and archangels, our theater of worship calls, at the very least, for reverent agnosticism on the subject. At best it calls upon us to enter reverently the presence of the Creator of all that is, acknowledging that much of what is real is unseen by us. It calls upon us to worship the One whom we call Father, Son, and Holy Spirit.

The doctrine of the Trinity, I have argued in this first part of our study, is fundamental to an understanding of Christian worship. God the Spirit empowers it. God the Son initiates it. And God the Father creates us with the capacity freely to respond to his bottomless love with our whole selves, in joy and thanksgiving. Our understanding of God as one in being, but with diversity in that unity, adds one further essential insight into the nature of true worship. The activity of worship is also characterized by unity in diversity and diversity in unity. We turn now to explore some of the multifaceted diversity of unified Christian response to God.

Part Two
THE BODY AT WORSHIP

5

WE GATHER TOGETHER

Sunday morning is a strange piece of the week. For many Christians it is the time to gather together in a special place—"to go to church." We assemble in Christ's name at that time and in that space for an activity we call worship. For many of our neighbors it is a time for another kind of freedom from everydayness—a time to cut loose from the demands of the workaday week. Sunday morning provides space for self-indulgence and for self-realization, a space for sleeping late and then reading all the sections of the Sunday newspaper.

We begin thinking about the rich diversity of Christian worship patterns by focusing on the first day of the week. It is a day we now consider part of the weekend, but that word "weekend" has been in the English language for only about a hundred years. Early Christians thought of Sunday as the start of a new week. They also called it "the Eighth Day." For them Sunday was connected as much to the future as to the past.

Two twentieth-century poets who used the term "Sunday morning" in titles of their poems caught its timeless spirit for modern secularists. In 1920, T. S. Eliot wrote of his own "Sunday Morning Service"—his morning tub. His Sweeney "shifts from ham to ham stirring the water in his bath," while the unoffending feet of the baptized God

shine through "water pale and thin." In the same generation and in the same vein, Wallace Stevens painted a lazy
Sunday morning in female dress. "Complacencies of the
peignoir" mingle with "late coffee and oranges in a sunny
chair" to dissipate "the holy hush of ancient sacrifice."

That line, "the holy hush of ancient sacrifice," pinpoints
a major problem in the history of the chief day of Christian
worship. We confused the first day of the week with the
Jewish Sabbath and thereby turned to the past instead of
to the future. Rightly understood, Sunday is more a day of
tension than a day of rest.

The confusion is sadly reflected in a chapter of the 1643
Westminster Confession titled "Of Religious Worship and
the Sabbath Day." John Calvin's own discussion of the
commandment, "Remember the Sabbath Day to keep it
holy," does not show the same hardening of spiritual arter-
ies that afflicted the Westminster divines. Calvin extolled
the Sabbath Day as a chance for believers to cease from
their own work so that God could work in them. He also
saw it as a day for training in piety and as a chance to give
the servants a day off. He took a rather cavalier view of
which day of the week should be set aside for such purposes. He thought that was only a "politic arrangement."
Presumably Wednesday would have done as well as Sunday.

For his successors in the Reformed tradition, on the
other hand, Sunday morning was set apart by "a positive
and perpetual commandment . . . to be continued to the
end of the world as the Christian Sabbath." All "worldly
employments and recreations" were to be set aside. The
whole time was to be devoted to public and private exercises of worship or to works of mercy. A holy hush of duty
descended on one seventh of our lives and suffocated a
great deal of Christian joy. Instead of energized anticipation of Easter dawn, we were left with blue laws and
boredom.

We need to go back to earlier tradition to recapture the keen on-tiptoe feeling that Christians used to have on the first day of the week. That day was not without some of the features that you and I still experience as part of our Sundays, it must be admitted. In Corinth in the middle of the first century the Christians knew about a collection of money: "On the first day of every week, each of you is to put something aside and store it up, as he may prosper, so that contributions need not be made when I come" (I Cor. 16:2). On "the first day of the week" in Troas, Christians encountered overlong and boring sermons. Paul once preached so interminably there that a young man named Eutychus fell asleep, fell out of the window, fell to his death (Acts 20:7ff.). Until, of course, Paul raised him up.

What set the first day of the week apart in the early church, and made it a day that was tensely alive, was its connection both with Jesus' resurrection and with his anticipated, imminent return in great glory. All four Gospels use the phrase "the first day of the week" in their accounts of the resurrection. The wording in Matthew underlines the distinction from the Sabbath: "Now after the sabbath, toward the dawn of the first day of the week, Mary Magdalene and the other Mary went to see the sepulchre. And behold . . ." (Matt. 28:1). Mark and Luke also emphasize the fact that the Sabbath was past when the women went to the tomb on the first day of the week. Although John's timing of the crucifixion is different, he also uses the crucial phrase: "Now on the first day of the week Mary Magdalene came to the tomb early, while it was still dark . . ." (John 20:1).

From the very first, Christian worship was celebration of the resurrection. The time of Christian worship was the day of resurrection, the dawn of the new creation, the first day of the New Age. When the fathers reflected theologically on the time of worship, they repeatedly made the point that Sunday is the day of new beginnings. As the first day of the week, Sunday was and is the symbol of the beginning of all things.

When the primitive church called Sunday also the eighth day, however, it cast a spotlight not only on the first Easter but also on the consummation of history, expected at any moment. It would be the end of time as we know it, the beginning of eternity. Eager yearning for Christ's return in glory is hard for us to understand. For us a week has only seven days. We have trouble with the symbol of an eighth. In his powerful 1967 novel, *The Eighth Day,* Thornton Wilder managed nevertheless to break open the symbolism for us by means of a simple typographical trick. The last line of his novel wears no final period. It just opens out into the future.

The earliest Christian document to talk about Sunday as the eighth day is the Epistle to Barnabas, which has been well described as a sort of "poor relation" to the Epistle to the Hebrews. Although the work once had a chance of becoming part of the New Testament canon, the early church wisely decided it did not deserve to be included. Yet it has historical importance for its argument that at the end of time when the Son comes again, he will make "the beginning of an eighth day, that is, the beginning of another world." "Wherefore," the writer continues, "we also celebrate with gladness the eighth day in which Jesus also rose from the dead."

Reading about our ancestors' understanding of the eighth day is like trying to play some kind of numbers game in an unknown language. We cannot count theologically in the same way that Justin Martyr, Basil the Great, and Augustine counted. Yet they can all help us recapture the future orientation native to the first day of the week, understood simultaneously as an eighth.

For Justin Martyr in the mid-second century, eighth-day language had an important connection with Jesus' circumcision and hence with baptism. Jesus was circumcised when he was eight days old. In the early church, Christians were baptized only on Sunday, and in some places only on Easter. Hence, as Justin Martyr sees it, when Christians receive Christ's name, it is on the same day Jesus received his name, that is, the eighth. Associations such as this explain why the oldest baptistries and the oldest baptismal fonts are octagonal in shape.

According to Basil, in his fourth-century treatise on the Holy Spirit, we stand up to pray on Sunday "because that day is in some way the image of the future age." Standing is an active posture. It is the posture of one who has been resurrected. The soaring vision of Augustine expanded on this idea at the end of his great work on the theology of history, *The City of God*. The Sabbath is brought to a close not by an evening, he said, "but by the Lord's day, as an eighth and eternal day, consecrated by the resurrection of Christ, and also prefiguring the eternal repose not only of the spirit, but also of the body. Then we shall rest and see, see and love, love and praise. This is what shall be in the end without end."

We could not revive these ancient names for Sunday— First Day and Eighth Day—even if we wanted to; but they do teach us at least two important things about our time for worship. The first is simply that Sunday morning is a time of joy. Each and every Sunday is an Easter. Each and every Sunday is a time for celebrating God's triumphant victory over all the forces of darkness and death. It is a time for affirming light and life. Whatever else we may do in worship, chiefly we are freed to praise God for the glorious resurrection of his Son, Jesus Christ.

The second is that Sunday is a time of re-creation, of new beginning. It is the start of a new week, a week that has never been before nor will ever come again. Sunday is pregnant with the possibilities of the week. So Sunday is a time to look forward, to welcome the new. It is a day on which we celebrate the power of the Spirit to transform

even us, in order that we may become agents in the trans-
formation of God's world.

The phrase "to go to church" makes it necessary to think
also about the place of our worship. The church, of course,
is not a building on the corner of Main Street. It is that
body of people of whom Christ is the head. Nevertheless
the places where Christians assemble give visible expression to the fact that we are called out to be God's people.
And the buildings in which we meet speak their own symbolic language. Four examples from the wide variety of
buildings used for worship will help us focus on the mean-
ings of our spaces—the house, the basilica, the cathedral,
and the "storefront" church.

First, the house. In New Testament times someone's
house was the primary place in which to gather on the
Lord's Day. In his letters Paul names two men and two
women who had "churches" in their houses—Aquila and
Prisca (I Cor. 16:19; Rom. 16:5), Nympha (Col. 4:15), and
Philemon (Philemon 2). Presumably these were people
relatively well-off, with enough room in their houses to
accommodate at least a small gathering of brothers and
sisters. We know almost nothing about them as individuals
beyond the accounts in Acts concerning Aquila and Prisca
(or Priscilla). Intriguingly, they are both reported to have
taken Apollos aside, after he had spoken boldly in the
synagogue in Ephesus, and expounded to him "the way of
God more accurately" (Acts 18:26). Surely this account is
one of the earliest records of direct "feedback" for a Christian preacher.

Houses used for worship make two noteworthy symbolic
statements about Christian understanding of place. On
the one hand, they announce that the human occupants
are more important than the site. Pauline language further underlines this fact when Paul tells the Ephesians:
"So then you are no longer strangers and sojourners, but
you are fellow citizens with the saints and members of the

household of God" (Eph. 2:19). The Ephesians are *personally* the dwelling place of God in the Spirit, *themselves* growing into a holy temple in the Lord. On the other hand, houses simultaneously announce that no place is any longer profane—in the root sense of outside the sacred precincts of the Temple. All places are hallowed by the presence of God.

Second, the basilica. A basilica was simply a large oblong public building in ancient Rome, a place for public assembly and often for a court of justice. After the emperor Constantine's recognition of their religion in the fourth century, Christians increasingly erected such buildings to use for their assemblies. This development testifies not only to the growing numbers of Christians, so that they could no longer fit into someone's living room, but also to that reconciliation with the state which made Christianity dangerously respectable, whatever the compensations for such success.

St. Peter's Basilica in Rome may well be the best-known symbol of that ambiguous triumph of Christendom. The Michelin guidebook to Italy says baldly that that basilica is "the most majestic building in the world." Such language seems particularly appropriate when one remembers that the architectural term "basilica" derives from the Greek word for king, *basileus.* We are reminded of the biblical affirmation that God is King of the universe for whose universal Kingdom we pray.

Third, the cathedral. Again the root meaning of the word is instructive, coming as it does from the Latin for "chair." Strictly speaking, a cathedral is the official seat of the bishop of a diocese. But the symbolic significance of this sort of building as a place of worship goes far beyond any form of ecclesiastical polity.

Consider a thirteenth-century Gothic cathedral such as that at Chartres, for example. Artists and craftsmen and common laborers joined together to express in such a structure their common faith, offering to God their skill and their labor and their devotion. For such a structure, human beings took the material stuff of creation—stone and sand and wood and metal—and transformed it to show forth the beauty of holiness. Countless pilgrims and tourists praying in that place through the centuries since added spiritual resonance. Now the very stones themselves seem to sing the praises of God. Who is to say that those costly materials should have been sold and the money given to the poor?

But, finally, an inner-city "storefront" church also speaks a symbolic language. And it too can bespeak the beauty of holiness. It is there, in that place where people are in need. It usually has a large plate-glass window opening onto the sidewalk. People passing by know it as a place of worship, even if the church cannot afford a neon sign to announce the fact. People inside can readily look out on the world for which Christ died. People outside will be warmly welcomed if they come in—even without wearing Sunday clothes. Here the mission of the church is inescapably visible.

Clearly it is as easy to sentimentalize a storefront church, which is probably scrabbling to keep the rent paid, as it is to sentimentalize a Gothic cathedral. Both have known human ugliness, even human murder. Nevertheless we need to include storefronts as well as cathedrals in our lexicon of holy space, basilicas as well as the houses we live in day by day.

We Christians gather to worship at special times—usually on Sunday morning. We gather to worship in special places—more often in an ordinary urban or suburban or country church than in any of the kinds of buildings we have just been thinking about. The paint may well be peeling. The heating bills are probably worrisome. Yet it is our place, our space for praising the God who created and encountered and consecrated time and space. For that reason we join our voices with the whole company of heaven in giving thanks to God. For that is a good and joyful thing to do, as the ancient prayer puts it, "at all times, and in all places."

6

SERVING THE WORD

When Christians come together each Lord's Day, they come as heirs of Judaism. The greatest single legacy the first Christians received from the worship of their ancestors was the centrality of the Book. Even as reading and expounding Scripture was the major focus in the synagogue of Nazareth in Jesus' day, so reading and expounding Scripture became a major focus of Christian worship. It still is.

Act one of the drama of Christian worship as many of us know it can be outlined in three simple scenes. After some praise and some prayers, someone stands up and reads from something we call the Old Testament. In scene two, one or more passages are read from something we call the New Testament. Then, in scene three, a person we recognize as a duly authorized leader mounts a pulpit, usually an elevated platform, and talks about those readings. We sit and listen.

This is the basic structure of what is sometimes called the Service of the Word. In earlier days it was known as the Mass of the Catechumens, because even nonbaptized persons were permitted to share in this part of worship. In earlier days also, such as those of Augustine of Hippo, there was another notable difference. He sat down to preach. The people stood and listened. They had no pews in their church.

However familiar we may be with this scenario, it is far more complicated than it seems. We need to ask about the readers as well as about the readings. What are the readers doing? We need to ask about the preacher as well as about the sermon. What is she or he doing? What is the sermon about? And we need to ask about those men and women sitting in the pews listening. What are they hearing?

Reading is such an everyday activity for most people in our society that we easily forget that millions of people in the world are illiterate today, and that for centuries in the past also only a small minority were able to read. In the Middle Ages, even private reading was a physical activity. One pronounced the words with the lips, audibly. In monastic culture, as Don Jean Leclercq has shown, the *act* of reading Holy Scripture, the *lectio divina,* was associated with *ruminatio,* chewing on the sacred text until it was thoroughly digested. A devout monk was praised because "his mouth ruminated the sacred words" without resting.

Public reading of Holy Scripture was for centuries the privilege of the lector, considered a member of one of the minor orders by the Roman Catholic Church. In the service ordaining a new lector, the bishop charged him: "Apply yourself, therefore, to speaking the word of God, the sacred lessons, clearly, audibly, and without alteration, that the faithful may be enlightened and edified and that the truth of the divine lessons be never corrupted through thy fault."

This charge could equally well be addressed to men and women today who read the lessons in worship. They too are reading "the word of God" so that the congregation may be enlightened and built up. The role of the reader is to be the person through whom God speaks to the assembled worshipers. Inevitably any reading aloud is an act of interpretation. Yet the voice of the reader is only the voice of the prophet, in the root sense of that biblical term. Readers are spokespersons for the Lord, with the Lord's word in their mouths.

From the first, Christians read from the Hebrew Scriptures in their worship. In the earliest years Christians had only the two sections of the Jewish canon known to Jesus, "the law and the prophets." In Greek-speaking congregations these lessons were read in translation, from the Septuagint, or Greek version of Scripture. Gradually, even before the close of the New Testament period, Christian writings were also read aloud. Paul directs the Colossians to have his letter read out among them and then to have it read also in Laodicea (Col. 4:16). By the time II Peter was written, Paul's letters are themselves spoken of as Scripture (II Peter 3:16). The Christian community was in the process of adding a canon of "New Covenant" writings to those they retained from the "Old Covenant" which God made with Israel. The end result is the collection of sixty-six different writings, originally in Hebrew or Aramaic or Greek, which we call the Bible. Printed in relatively small type, in English translation they come to more than twelve hundred pages. How do we decide which pages to read aloud in worship? And how do we decide in what language to read them?

Both issues were important ones at the time of the Reformation. The early advocates of reform, such as John Wycliffe, insisted that the Scriptures are divinely inspired in all their parts, and therefore equally authoritative throughout. They also insisted that all Christians should read and hear them in their own native language. Although Martin Luther, in the preface to the first edition of his German New Testament, was willing to admit that some books in it are better and nobler than others, he was equally adamant that the Scripture must be in the vernacular. People should hear the word of God in the same language they use every day at home and work.

One solution to the first question, that of what parts of Scripture we read in worship, is that suggested by Wycliffe. Since it is all equally important, read it all straight through. Start with Gen. 1:1 and Matt. 1:1 and continue reading in course. Another solution, at the opposite extreme, is to read whatever portions of Scripture seem to be appropriate to the concerns of the congregation or to the themes of the preacher on any given Sunday.

A large proportion of Christendom, and an increasing proportion in recent years, has chosen a solution midway between these extremes of form and freedom—the solution of a lectionary, a fixed selection of biblical readings geared to the church year. As far as readings from the Epistles and the Gospels are concerned, this solution goes back at least as far as the seventh century, the date of the oldest extant liturgical lectionary. The idea of a lectionary is increasingly winning ecumenical approval in our day, to such an extent that on the same Sunday millions of us are now hearing the same parts of the Bible read and expounded.

The use of a lectionary has at least two major advantages over reading straight through a given book, including all the genealogical tables and cultic laws of ancient Israel, or listening only to the pastor's favorite passages. It more readily relates the readings to one another, so that the Old Testament lesson illuminates the New, and the New enriches the Old. It also powerfully invites us to enter into the annual cycle commemorating the mighty acts of God in Christ.

Our common discovery in recent years that Christians can share a common lectionary is probably one of the greatest contributions to church unity in our time. The attendant reemphasis on the Christian year, starting with Advent and progressing through the Sundays after Pentecost, is an equally important gift to Christian self-under-standing. We worship as members of one body, in spite of our unhappy divisions. We worship as a people on the move toward the future consummation of God's purpose already inaugurated in the birth, life, death, and resurrec-tion of Jesus Christ. Liturgical readings selected to accord with these great themes year by year both celebrate God's action and deepen the hearers' commitment to the Way.

The issue of which language to use, however, remains a lively one in current discussion of worship. Not everyone who accepts the Reformation principle that Scripture should be read in words readily understood by the congre-gation is willing to forgo the great cadences of the King James Version. Surely "she brought forth butter in a lordly dish" sounds better than "she brought him curds in a lordly bowl" (Judg. 5:25). Even if some people no longer realize that "prevent" really means "precede" (I Thess. 4:15), we should not abandon our lofty heritage for the pedestrian prose of a modern translation, some say. Nor is everyone agreed that when Paul used the word *adelphoi*, he really meant "brothers *and* sisters" since he included women among those whom he greeted in that manner. After all, *adelphoi* means just "brothers."

Strong and often bitter feelings on such matters of bibli-cal translation indicate the continuing need for Christians to take words seriously. As a people who know God through the revelation of the incarnate Word, Jesus the Christ, we dare not be careless in our use of language. Often the reader, after announcing the lesson, charges the hearers, "Listen for the word of God!" It is increasingly difficult for many women to hear God's word addressed to them after their "ears have popped," as one such woman aptly put it. When they are invited to think of themselves as sons of God and brothers in Christ, they just hear a door slammed in their faces.

The answer to this dilemma may lie, in part, in the

development of a common lectionary that is a somewhat freer translation of the readings, approaching more nearly a paraphrase faithful to the intent of the authors, rather than a strict word-by-word translation of the Greek or Hebrew. Such an experiment, at least, currently has the approval of the National Council of Churches which bears responsibility for the Revised Standard Version of the Bible. Council members are agreed that the Bible is the living word of God. It must come alive in the ears and minds and hearts of the faithful.

To help make it come alive is one of the chief jobs of the preacher. The sermon which follows the lessons is the means whereby their message is proclaimed for our day and for our situation. Sometimes this may involve denunciation as well as annunciation, as liberation theologians such as Gustavo Gutiérrez argue. Comfortable, well-fed Christians in the pews need to hear God's word of judgment as well as the good news of forgiveness. Sometimes this may mean explanation as well as exhortation. People in the pews are thirsty for a deeper understanding of the faith as well as for growing power to know and obey God's will.

Fashions in sermons change from generation to generation, both in length and in style, much like hemlines and neckties. England's York Minster used to keep an hourglass in the pulpit so that the preacher would stop after sixty minutes. Seminarians today learn that no one is ever saved after twenty minutes, and most parishioners would like to cut the time to twelve.

In sixteenth-century Geneva, John Calvin usually preached twice on Sunday and, in alternate weeks, once every weekday as well. He expounded the Bible reading, phrase by phrase. He believed that God encountered people and enlivened their faith through such exposition of the text. In seventeenth-century England great preachers like John Donne and Jeremy Taylor embellished their preaching with such poetic diction that students of English literature read their sermons to this day. By the eighteenth century, when rationalism invaded the churches, a sermon became much like a lecture, judged by the cogency of its arguments and the precision of its logic.

The sermon has suffered from similar changes of fashion in twentieth-century America as well. For a time the Protestant pulpit seemed to be the anteroom of the psychiatrist's office. More recently it has seemed to move closer once again to the scriptural norm set in Calvin's Geneva.

In his 1929 play, *The Green Pastures*, exploring what we would now call the black religious experience, Marc Connelly has a delightful conversation between God and Noah. At one point in the conversation Noah says to God: "I'm jes' ol' preacher Noah, Lawd, an' I'm yo' servant. I ain' very much, but I'se all I got." All preachers would do well to heed the first part of these lines and deny the last part. Preachers may not think very highly of their homiletical skill, but if they are servants of the Lord, that is enough. It is not true that they are all they've got. God the Spirit has promised to teach them what to say.

At its core, worship is dialogic. The lessons read and heard constitute a dialogue between God and the congregation, through the voice of the reader and the ears of the listeners. The sermon preached and heard constitutes a dialogue between God and his people, through the voice of the preacher and the ears of the listeners. Without those ears, the Service of the Word, however eloquent the reading and however inspired the preaching, remains a noisy gong and a clanging cymbal. No dialogue, no true worship can occur.

The prophets of Israel indict those who have ears and hear not. Jesus repeatedly healed the deaf, and the Evangelists mean us to understand that figuratively as well as literally. Both strands of our biblical tradition should alert us to the importance of right listening and right hearing in Christian worship. Right listening is an art. Right hearing is a gift.

Almost all of us when listening have looked impatiently at our watches or simply "turned off" during long, dull sermons. We need not feel overly guilty about this. The art of listening demands our energized attention, our openness to hearing new things, perhaps painful things, certainly amazing things. But it also allows us to take off on our own tangent, to hear our individual messages. We should not listen to either lessons or sermons as if we were tape recorders. Listening is a responsive art. We are creative agents in this dialogue.

Almost all of us listening to Scripture and sermons have also had the experience, however rare, of hearing new things. Suddenly the light bulbs flash on, the bells ring, and we know something we did not know before—whether it be about ourselves or our world or our God. That gift of opened ears and hearts is not something we can program simply by leaning forward in our pews during the Service of the Word, straining to pay attention. Rather, it is a gift experienced while letting go and letting God address us.

7

MAKING EUCHARIST

Act two of the drama of Christian worship also has a simple structure, but in four scenes instead of three. The four scenes are outlined in four verbs repeated emphatically in several New Testament accounts: Jesus *took* bread and *blessed* it; he *broke* it and *gave* it to his disciples.

In this chapter we will be thinking about the Lord's Supper, the most distinctive act of Christian worship and the essential complement, many Christians believe, to the Service of the Word. For centuries both together constituted the principal worship on the Lord's Day, whether called The Divine Liturgy, as in Eastern Orthodox churches, or The Mass or The Eucharist, as in Western churches.

The oldest description we have of the institution of the Lord's Supper comes in the middle of Paul's letter telling the Christians at Corinth how they should behave in worship: "For I received from the Lord what I also delivered to you, that the Lord Jesus on the night when he was betrayed took bread, and when he had given thanks, he broke it, and said, 'This is my body which is for you. Do this in remembrance of me'" (I Cor. 11:23–24). The claim to have received this command "from the Lord" is merely a claim that there is an unbroken line of tradition going back to Jesus' last supper with his disciples. Some scholars think that Paul was handing on this tradition as he himself had learned it in Antioch about A.D. 40.

With minor variations each of the Synoptic Gospels recounts the institution of the Lord's Supper. Matthew 26: 26, Mark 14:22, and Luke 22:19 each use the four verbs for the four distinct actions of Jesus. The words reoccur in Luke's story of the way in which two disciples recognize the risen Lord at the supper table in Emmaus (Luke 24: 30). The Fourth Gospel does not contain a similar report at the time of the Last Supper. Instead, John emphasizes Jesus' washing of the disciples' feet. Yet the same actions are underscored in his description of the feeding of the multitude (John 6:11), just preceding the discourse on Jesus as the Bread of Life.

Jesus took bread, and after supper, in the Pauline version, he took the cup "in the same way." This action of taking became from very early times in the life of the church the occasion of the people's offering. Justin Martyr's *Apology,* written almost one hundred years after Paul's directions to Corinth, makes it clear that the worshipers brought bread and wine from home. At the end of the second century, in the time of Hippolytus, who gives us the oldest full outline of the liturgy in existence, the people brought not only bread and wine but other foodstuffs as well. These too were offered to the Lord and later distributed to the poor. Today, along with bread and wine, Christians offer money, the symbolic fruit of their life and labor.

The Offertory, as this part of the service is traditionally called, makes at least two essential, if largely nonverbal, statements about the relationship between God and the people of God. It acknowledges that everything anyone has comes as a gift from the Creator. It expresses our responsive role as nothing less than cocreators with God, in whose image we are made.

As a result of the modern liturgical movement, one

often witnesses an offertory procession in which men and women carry forward from the midst of the congregation bread and wine and dollar bills all at the same time. Once again we encounter the fact that nothing is profane in Christian understanding. The "sacred elements" of bread and wine, as they are sometimes called, belong together with the money. It is appropriate that the people often stand and say: "All things come of thee, O Lord."

Bread and wine, however, represent the raw materials of nature in the form of human manufacture. Someone grew the grain. Someone baked the bread. Someone carefully treated the juice from the grapes. The food and drink carried forward up a church aisle are the produce of human property and the products of human labor.

The noted liturgical scholar Massey H. Shepherd, Jr., once said that if the laity really understood the meaning of the Offertory in the Eucharist, and the way in which they are involved in it, no one would have to worry about Christian witness in the social issues of modern life. When we offer to God these symbols of labor and property, our major preoccupations for six days out of seven, we are asking that our work and our property may become redemptive instruments to build true community among all sorts and conditions of human beings.

In the late 1960s a left-wing Roman Catholic priest expressed the connection between the eucharistic Offertory and Christian social action even more graphically. He was a member of a Manhattan community which called itself Emmaus House. The community published a magazine entitled *The Bread Is Rising,* a phrase that was alleged to be a password whispered by peasants at the time of the French Revolution. At their eucharistic liturgy a loaf of bread and a bottle of Chianti were set upon the table. At the Offertory the group, packed close together around the table, sang a song called "A Little Help from My Friends." In those days it was, of course, accompanied by guitar. As

quoted in *The New Yorker*, the priest in charge said that
liturgical experimentation is not enough. "The true gospel
of the poor is better housing. . . . Picketing is a form of
praying." He added, "Praying, after all, is a form of picketing."

After the Offertory comes the great prayer of thanksgiving, the second major action. In the light of contemporary
ecumenical discussion of this prayer, traditionally called
the Prayer of Consecration, three observations must be
made. Each of them has been the subject of much contro-
versy among Christians; but each is now, I believe, the
subject of widespread agreement. Ecumenical dialogue
has made enormous strides in recent decades.

First, the thanksgiving rightly uses a wide-angle lens.
The focus is not just on what Christ did and said on the
night in which he was betrayed, nor even just on his crucifixion and resurrection. It goes back in thanks for all of
God's mighty acts in creation and redemption, thanks for
his work in all the galaxies as well as on this planet. It looks
forward in keen anticipation to his coming again in power
and great glory. Thus all times and all places are here
made explicitly the arena of thanksgiving.

Second, the prayer traditionally includes a recitation of
Christ's words of institution at the Last Supper: "This is my
body . . . ," "This is my blood . . ."; but it also includes a
specific invocation of God the Holy Spirit, asking his active
involvement in the lives of the worshipers as well as in and
through the offered bread and wine. In this perspective
there is no room for the old polemic charge of hocus-
pocus, the charge of a magical interpretation of the words
"Hoc est corpus meum." No responsible theologian today
believes, if indeed any ever did, that the priest's recitation
of the words "This is my body . . ." is the effective agent
in making Christ present in the Eucharist.

The third observation is closely related. Debates over
sacramental theology used to center around the mode of

Christ's presence in the so-called consecrated elements. Was he present in the bread and wine, after the words had been recited, by the mode of transubstantiation or consubstantiation or in some undefined way known as "Real Presence"? Or just in the hearts of faithful believers as they ate the bread and drank of the cup?

In recent years we have broken loose from those fences around our understanding. We now talk of the various modes of Christ's presence with us—in the plural. He is in the midst of all of us as we gather in his name, just as he promised he would be. He is present in his word, read and proclaimed. He is present through the ordained person who presides in his name. He is present also through the bread and cup eaten and drunk in remembrance of him. What matters is that God in Christ *is* present. And so we give thanks.

Next, the bread is broken. In this third action of this part of the liturgy, we once again encounter multileveled symbolism, a powerful conflation of basic Christian themes. If we listen to the book of Acts, very early Christians used this act of breaking—this Fraction, to use the traditional technical term—as a proper name for the whole Lord's Supper. The newly baptized, Acts says, devoted themselves "to the apostles' teaching and fellowship, to the breaking of bread and the prayers" (Acts 2:42). A few verses later they are described as attending the Temple together and "breaking bread in their homes" (Acts 2:46).

Breaking bread together remains a powerful metaphor for our sharing of ourselves. It is an idiom for hospitality and for mutual trust. According to the second-century document called *The Didache,* or the Teaching of the Twelve Apostles, the stress at the fraction was on prior and future gatherings: "As this broken bread was scattered upon the mountains and being gathered became one, so may thy Church be gathered together from the ends of the earth into thy kingdom." Paul sounds a similar note of

Christian unity when he asks: "The bread which we break, is it not a participation in the body of Christ? Because there is one bread, we who are many are one body, for we all partake of the one bread" (I Cor. 10:16–17). The custom in some churches of feeding communicants little round individual wafers, showing no sign of brokenness and hence no sign of oneness, fails to convey this dimension of the symbolic action.

Breaking bread which is recognized as Christ's body also symbolizes, of course, the breaking of his human body on the cross. The word "sacrifice" has such a battle-scarred record in the history of Protestant-Catholic debate about the Eucharist that it is now likely to be relegated to a diplomatic footnote in bilateral agreements about the doctrine of the Lord's Supper. We no longer enjoy waving red flags in each other's faces. Nevertheless, when we are thinking about the breaking of the bread as a symbol of Christ's self-offering on the cross, the word "sacrifice" is not inappropriate. Through the *anamnesis,* the active remembrance of what he did, the recalling into the present of his once for all decisive self-giving, we become participants in that event, partakers of Calvary as well as of Easter.

The author of Hebrews puts it in the form of an invitation still appropriate to every breaking of the bread in Christian worship: "So Jesus also suffered outside the gate in order to sanctify the people through his own blood. Therefore let us go forth to him outside the camp, bearing abuse for him" (Heb. 13:12–13). Essential to the drama of Christian worship, deeply a part of its basic movement, is this dialectic of coming in and going out, of bringing bread in thanksgiving to God so that it may be, so that we may be, fractured. In his name.

The fourth verb in the scenario for the second act we are considering is *gave.* Even as Jesus gave the broken bread to his disciples, so now the broken bread is distributed among the faithful, and likewise the wine. The people eat and drink together.

The mystery of all of life is focused in this Sacrament of bread and wine. In one sense, therefore, the most appropriate response is that expressed in the hymn from the Liturgy of St. James, "Let all mortal flesh keep silence, and with fear and trembling stand." Nevertheless, we need to affirm at least three of the many dimensions of this climactic symbolic act of worship.

Eating and drinking are such commonplace, everyday activities that we seldom think very deeply about them in connection with this particular eating and drinking which some call "Holy Communion." But precisely such a connection with all our other meals is made explicit at this service when, shortly before sharing the bread and wine, the congregation says together the petition Jesus taught: "Give us today our daily bread."

It follows not only that every meal is an occasion for thanksgiving, but that every meal is also an occasion for remembering the physical needs of others. Real hunger and real thirst are ever-present realities for a large portion of the world's population. Jesus' compassion for the multitudes who have nothing to eat, so well attested in all the Gospels, is necessarily shared by all those who participate in this communion with him.

Yet this eating and drinking speak equally to that spiritual hunger and thirst which all of us share, even immediately after a full dinner. Such hunger and thirst are master metaphors at the heart of Jesus' teaching. "Blessed are those who hunger and thirst for righteousness, for they shall be satisfied" (Matt. 5:6). Or again, in his dialogue with the Samaritan woman at the well, "Every one who drinks of this water will thirst again, but whoever drinks of the water that I shall give him will never thirst" (John 4: 13–14). So this drinking and eating in worship are simultaneously thanksgiving for "the fountain of the water of life" (Rev. 21:6), the new life in Christ Jesus.

And therefore this eating and drinking are also a participation now in the feast of the future. The idea of a Messianic banquet was a major feature of first-century thought about the end time. The connection with the coming of the Kingdom is made by Jesus himself in the Gospel accounts of the Last Supper. That thrust toward the future is reiterated by Paul when he tells the Corinthians: "For as often as you eat this bread and drink the cup, you proclaim the Lord's death until he comes" (I Cor. 11:26). "Maranatha," "Our Lord, come!" ended the thanksgiving after the eucharistic meal in some parts of the primitive church. But those who had eaten and drunk with him in that meal knew his presence already in their midst, knew a foretaste of that future fulfillment.

Banquet imagery is unlikely to play a very large part in our dreams of the future today. The very idea of a banquet conjures up in the minds of many of us thoughts of tough broiled chicken, cold green peas, and boring after-dinner speeches. But in an age when many of us wonder whether there is any future to hope for, the Eucharist is nevertheless the solid food of hope. Because it binds us to the Christ with whom we keep the feast, it nourishes us with steadfast hope in God's promise to be forever with his people.

8

REACHING OUT

Next to God, the principal actors in this two-act drama of Christian worship are the men, women, and children in the pews. We all have energetic roles to play. We cannot sit passively, as an audience might. We have to reach out and move out. Without such action on the part of the people, the whole enterprise of corporate worship would be futile. Liturgy, after all, simply means public work. And worshipers have the Lord's work to do.

In addition to gathering, listening, and feasting, Christians at worship sing and pray, touch and leave. And each of these actions also plays an essential part in their relationship with God, with each other, and with the world. We need now to think about hymnody, intercession, the Peace, and the dismissal as ingredients of Sunday worship.

The Westminster Larger Catechism begins with a classic definition of what it means to be human. Our "chief and highest end is to glorify God, and fully to enjoy him forever." One of the chief ways in which we glorify God, although by no means the only one, is through singing hymns of praise in our worship together.

Glory is one of those religious words which few of us can define very clearly. The Greek word that is translated "glory" is *doxa,* from which we get Doxology as a name for

such familiar hymns as "Praise God from whom all bless-
ings flow." The Old Testament word most frequently
translated "glory" means heavy, weighty. We mean something similar when we speak of a person who carries a
good deal of weight, not meaning a person who is obese
but someone to whom we pay attention because of the
person's power or achievements. "Glory" and "splendor"
and "power" and "might" are all closely related terms; so
is "holiness."

When we glorify God in worship we are reminded that
God's glory is an awesome thing. The book of Exodus tells
us that when the Israelites saw the glory of the Lord set-
tling on Mt. Sinai the appearance of it was "like a devour-
ing fire" (Ex. 24:17). When the glory of the Lord shone
round the shepherds outside Bethlehem on that first
"Christmas Eve," they were "sore afraid" (Luke 2:9).
When Isaiah heard the seraphim singing in the Temple of
Jerusalem, however, he heard them declare that the
whole earth is full of God's glory (Isa. 6:3). And when the
Word became flesh and dwelt among us, according to the
prologue to the Fourth Gospel, we saw what God's glory
really looks like. For this reason Christians sing glory-
songs. Every hymnal is full of them. Indeed, a hymn properly so called is always a glory-song, an act of praise.

Along with the Service of the Word, Christians inherited the Psalter from Judaism. They have used it ever since
as a major sourcebook for their songs of worship. The word
"psalm" is, in fact, a dictionary synonym for the word
"hymn," so one can say accurately that the Psalter was the
hymnal that Jesus knew and used. He may well have
known much of it by heart, since he was probably quoting
from it on the cross.

The psalms, which for centuries constituted a large portion of the daily offices in every monastery in Europe,
provide many of our purest hymns of praise. Notable
among them is Psalm 95, the Venite:

> O come, let us sing to the LORD;
>   let us make a joyful noise to the rock of our
>   salvation!
> Let us come into his presence with thanksgiving;
>   let us make a joyful noise to him with songs
>   of praise.

Or the equally familiar Jubilate, Psalm 100:

> Make a joyful noise to the LORD, all the lands!
> Serve the Lord with gladness!
> Come into his presence with singing!

Many of our most cherished hymns are simply paraphrases of the biblical psalms, including John Milton's incomparable glory-song:

> Let us with a gladsome mind
> Praise the Lord, for he is kind.

If the Psalter is in any sense a model for hymnody today, however, we must sharply qualify the statement that a hymn by definition is a song of praise. For many of the psalms are psalms of lament. They protest against what has befallen the Jewish nation. They beseech God to deliver individuals from their pain and suffering. They lash out with such invective against their enemies, national and personal, that many modern Christians are uncomfortable about using parts of the Psalter in worship.

This dual character of Israel's psalmody is strikingly similar to the dual character of the spirituals of black Americans. James H. Cone, in his insightful book *The Spirituals and the Blues,* recognized the degree to which joy and despair were intertwined in the black religious experience. They were equally intertwined in Israel's religious experience. Nor is that paradoxical relationship foreign to the Christian understanding of the Christ who was glorified by being lifted on a cross.

Cone offers a magnificent example of this paradox of

hymnody and a superb comment on it. The spiritual is well known:

> Nobody knows the trouble I've seen,
> Nobody knows my sorrow.
> Nobody knows the trouble I've seen,
> Glory, Hallelujah!

Cone's comment captures the cruciform character of all Christian worship. "The 'Glory, Hallelujah!' is not a denial of trouble," he writes; "it is an affirmation of faith. God is the companion of sufferers, and *trouble* is not the last word on human existence" (p. 64).

A Franciscan once said: "A monk should own nothing but his harp." An old rabbinic saying, now posted on the wall of many a choir room across our land, declares that whoever sings prays twice. Both aphorisms recognize how completely one must invest oneself in any song if the singing is to gladden the heart and assuage one's sorrows. Christian hymnody is a way of going outside one's own skin, a way of energizing oneself to become truly a neighbor to the other. So is intercession.

A constant feature of Christian worship from its earliest days has been the prayers of the people for all sorts and conditions of humanity. Such prayers traditionally come between what we have called the two acts of the drama, between the Mass of the Catechumens and the Mass of the Faithful, to use old terminology. Are they, perhaps, rightly understood as an interlude—a necessary bridge between the proclamation of the Word and eucharistic response to great good news?

Whatever the proper position of these prayers in an outline of worship, they represent another means by which Christians get outside their own skins in worship, go beyond their own lives to pray for the whole church and the whole world. Through petition for the nations and their rulers, for the victims of injustice and oppression, for

homes and families, for the sick and the dying—all of life
is consciously brought before God.

Such intercession is often in the form of a litany, an
ancient pattern of dialogue prayer in which the leader
reads a short petition and the people make a fixed response. In such intercession, many Christians believe, a
local congregation joins consciously with the whole communion of saints, with all Christians everywhere. For
many, therefore, it seems fitting to pray with and for those
of past generations. At the time of the Reformation, however, abuses that were related to the Roman Catholic system of indulgences led many Protestants to reject all
prayer for the dead. Indeed the prayer book of the Church
of England at one time deliberately limited the scope of
intercession. The congregation heard the polemic bid-
ding: "Let us pray for the whole state of Christ's Church
militant here in earth."

"Intercessory prayer is not a scattering of good wishes
in the air," the missionary bishop Charles Brent once remarked; "it is the orderly operation of a vital energy, an
immediate transmitting of life." Through such prayer, he
believed, we become agents of power for others. God's
love, God's healing life, flows through us. It is, then, not a
matter of trying to change God's mind, as it were, but
rather of opening ourselves to be his servant people. As
members of the body of Christ, we draw near to God
through him who "always lives to make intercession"
(Heb. 7:25). Consequently we draw nearer to everyone
else in the human family.

This fact of drawing nearer to each other in worship is
frequently enacted visibly in the service by the exchange
of the Peace, an ancient practice lost to much modern
worship until the liturgical renewal of this century. In
some places this may be just a verbal exchange between
minister and people: "The peace of the Lord Jesus be with
you" and a response such as "And also with you." In many

other congregations a physical exchange of greeting is
growing in popularity. People shake hands, even hug one
another joyfully.

Introduction of the Peace has aroused extraordinary re-
sistance in some quarters. People, particularly perhaps
those of Anglo-Saxon background, show great reluctance
to touch each other "in public." But there are at least
three strong arguments for an active exchange of the
Peace. It is not just something liturgical that scholars want
to bring back to life out of antiquarian interest simply
because it was done in the primitive church. Rather, the
active reaching out to our neighbor recognizes that we are
embodied creatures, that we are Christians living toward
a vision, and that we are committed to moving from hostility to hospitality.

As embodied creatures, we engage in the public work
of worship with our full flesh-and-blood selves, not just
with our souls or with our minds. I have already insisted
on this fact of incarnation, but it bears repeating here.
What we say through body language is equally as important as what we say with our lips, in affecting both the
conscious and unconscious levels of our being. If I stretch
out my hand to you and you stretch out yours to me, if we
look at each other and touch each other, we are both
expressing and evoking a deeper interpersonal relationship—in the Lord. A deeper spiritual relationship, incar-
nated. We are practicing the fact that God has knit us
together in one communion and fellowship.

Living Toward a Vision (1976) is the felicitous title of
Walter Brueggemann's reflections on the biblical concept
of peace, of *shalom*. Two of the many scriptural passages
he cites are especially relevant to the action of exchanging
the Peace in the liturgy. First, the passage from Jeremiah
which reminds us that in the biblical vision of peace, actions speak louder than words. From prophet to priest,
says that great prophet, "they have healed the wound of

my people lightly, saying 'Peace, peace,' when there is no peace" (Jer. 6:14). Second, the announcement of a new state of affairs, the ringing proclamation of Eph. 2:13–14: "But now in Christ Jesus you who once were far off have been brought near in the blood of Christ. For he is our peace, who has made us both one, and has broken down the dividing wall of hostility."

Peace of the biblical kind, Brueggemann writes, is not simply a liturgical experience, "but one facing our deepest divisions and countering with a vision" (p. 24). One profound expression of that vision toward which we live is the vision of ministry enacted by Jesus at the Last Supper in John's Gospel. There the instruments of peace are not hardware but software. When Jesus washed his disciples' feet, he put *his* tools of ministry into our hands—a towel and a basin. A towel is not firm, but flexible, Brueggemann notes. It doesn't fit readily into our hands. "But then," he adds, "our hands must change and grow and become more flexible" (p. 135).

Moving from hostility to hospitality, a movement made possible by Christ according to the Ephesians passage just cited, is one of the three basic movements of the spiritual life, according to Henri Nouwen. In his influential little book *Reaching Out,* Nouwen sketches starkly the atmosphere of hostility in which we live most of the time. Not only do we fear hostility from strangers in the street, not only do we put dead bolts on our doors to keep intruders out, but we harbor a great deal of "backstage" hostility in ourselves. Nouwen challenges us to move from closed-in hostility to that attitude of hospitality whose roots are also deep in the biblical tradition, as deep as those of *shalom.*

"It belongs to the core of a Christian spirituality," he thinks, "to reach out to strangers and invite them into our lives" (p. 48). This requires creating a free and friendly space, one in which we open ourselves to new relationships, new friendships. In a world charged with hostility, each of us is called to be a healer. In Nouwen's judgment, careful attention by all members of the Christian community to such reaching out can often heal wounds before the special skills of priests or psychiatrists are needed.

A handshake, a hug in the midst of our worship, has the potentiality of bearing this kind of healing. It is one more way of going beyond ourselves into the world of God's tomorrow.

At the end of Sunday morning worship, we go home to get ready for Monday. This, too, is an essential action of the liturgy. We don't just leave. We are sent out. The dismissal does not write *finis* to a Sunday service. It commissions our daily service.

The name most widely used for the worship of Word and Sacrament which we have been thinking about is undoubtedly the Roman Catholic term, Mass. By some curious quirk of history, that name derives from the last words of the Latin liturgy, *"Ite, missa est."* On the surface level this simply means, "You are dismissed." Go home. It's finished. But on the deeper level it means mission; it means that you and I are sent forth to serve the Lord, Monday through Saturday, to be Christ's ministers in our places of work and in our places of play.

Contemporary liturgies use various forms of words, scriptural and nonscriptural, for the dismissal. But among the most incisive injunctions to the people are "Go out into the world in peace," and "Serve the Lord, rejoicing in the power of the Holy Spirit." If the peace with which we leave the church on Sunday morning is the biblical *shalom* we have been thinking about, we go forth as agents of justice and righteousness in the marketplaces of our towns and cities. God has commissioned us through our worship to be the instruments of his peace. If we go forth rejoicing in the power of the Holy Spirit, we go with great expectations, knowing that God can use even us to ease the world's pain.

Part Three
PRAYING PEOPLE

9

DISCIPLESHIP

So far I have been talking about worship as if it were primarily something Christians do together in a public place at a certain time each week. It is that. Yet the quality of our worship together is interdependent with the quality of our worship when we are apart. We need to think about our individual lives as praying people.

No Christian ever prays alone. Nevertheless, how each Christian prays in solitude, and how each Christian practices the presence of God, to use Brother Lawrence's classic phrase, makes a great difference in how well we pray together. In these final chapters we will focus on what is currently called Christian spirituality. The term is troublesome, because, as I argued in the preceding chapter, we are incarnate creatures, embodied selves—never pure spirits. Insofar as the term points to our conscious relationship with God, in the power of the Holy Spirit, however, it is a useful term. With that reference, I will use it to talk about our whole lives as lives of prayer.

Some years ago a disturbing book by Dietrich Bonhoeffer was published in English with the potent title *The Cost of Discipleship.* The book presented Bonhoeffer's meditations on the Sermon on the Mount, his understanding of Matthew 5–7. In it he used a stumbling-block phrase—one which for a time was quoted, it seemed, in three sermons out of every four. The phrase was "cheap grace." That is what we Christians have come to expect, Bonhoeffer claimed; but there is no such thing. Christian discipleship is costly. The fact that Bonhoeffer was subsequently executed by the Nazis because he tried to stop Hitler is not merely coincidental.

Discipleship sounds to many of us like an old-fashioned term. We are usually taught that a disciple is a follower. All of us as disciples are followers of the Way, followers of Jesus. This is true. But the word "disciples" also means pupils, learners. In this sense the cognate term "discipline" refers to any branch of learning—as in the discipline of physics or the discipline of psychology.

Such etymological notes can help launch us in our thinking about discipleship because they point toward the essential dimension of growth in understanding. No one of us has all the answers, or even all the right questions, about what it means to be a follower of Jesus. Yet each of us can learn from him, and from others who have followed him, about walking the road behind him.

As I understand the way such saints have trod, one must first think about one's total life-style before one can think constructively about personal prayer as such. The discipline *of* prayer emerges from a pattern of life which provides the support system, the discipline *for* prayer.

Anyone stung by Bonhoeffer's charge that we seek cheap grace may be tempted toward Christian romanticism at this point. With Sister Clare, we may think of abandoning our family, cutting off our hair, and joining Brother Francis in a life of holy poverty. But we know that the Lord has not endowed us with the courage for such a complete turnaround in our lives; and we do well to question whether he is asking that of all of us who are called to be disciples.

A saner, if less dramatic, call to discipleship is sounded

in the first lines of that old Shaker hymn which also speaks
of grace:

> 'Tis a gift to be simple, 'tis a gift to be free,
> 'Tis a gift to come down where we ought to be.

That text offers us a three-point charter for a Christian
life-style which can provide the disciplined background
for our prayer. We are called to simplicity and to freedom—in that spot on the map which God has assigned to
us.

Simplicity of life rejects the complicated, but it need not
mean homespun clothing and lots of yogurt. The gift of
being simple is not limited to natural-food fads or to
dowdy dress. It is the gift of being put-together, being
whole. In Nouwen's *Reaching Out,* it is the first of the
three essential movements of the spiritual life—that
reaching out to our own inmost selves which moves us
from loneliness to solitude. In the New Testament the
term "salvation" is closely related.

Simplicity of life means being straightforward. It is a gift
that affects the way we use our time and our money. It also
affects our personal relationships, so that we can be direct
in our dealings with other human beings, not manipula-
tive or conniving. In simplicity of life we can speak the
truth in love.

The issue of how we choose to use our time and our
money as Christians is an urgent one. It deserves our attention in a discussion of prayer and worship because it
concerns the ways in which we are responsive to God's gift
and call. Stewardship is not an item to be discussed only
at the time of an annual drive for funds. It measures the
way we till our gardens day by day.

Time is a major spiritual problem for contemporary
Christians. In spite of that great reordering of time which
we celebrate each Sunday and mark in our history with

the symbols B.C. and A.D., very few of us have made peace with our daily calendars and wristwatches. On the one hand, we feel harried and hurried and even hectic. On the other, we treat "busyness" as some kind of status symbol. How far in advance one has to invite a speaker or make a doctor's appointment is considered a sign of that person's success or even worth.

Our problem with time is not a new one. It is somehow comforting to know that it bothered seventeenth-century Christians, too. An anonymous prayer from that century reads, "Lord, temper with tranquillity our manifold activity, that we may do our work for thee with very great simplicity."

Simplicity of life demands stewardship of time. How any one of us learns to be a wise steward of our God-given weeks and days and hours and minutes is a highly individual matter. If we are to grow in discipleship, some time every day must be assigned to conscious, attentive encounter with God; but a surprising amount of prayer can take place at every stoplight or in the line at the bank or the supermarket. Some time surely needs to be assigned to attentive presence with family and friends, but some must also be left open for unscheduled encounter with our neighbors.

Money is also a major spiritual problem for contemporary Christians, whether we have too much of it, too little, or just a comfortable sufficiency. Next to wristwatches, checkbooks may pose a greater threat to our "immortal souls" than any other artifact in our consumer society. We are confronted on the one hand with Jesus' unequivocal command to one upright and responsible citizen: "Sell all that you have and distribute to the poor, and you will have treasure in heaven" (Luke 18:22). Holy poverty appears to be a hallmark of discipleship. But on the other hand we are told with equal clarity that each of us is to put something aside on the first day of the week, and store it up, as we may prosper, so that we may make our contribution to the saints (I Cor. 16:2).

In the face of this scriptural ambiguity, how are we to make responsible decisions about stewardship of money, as simplicity of life demands? No one has any easy answers, any pat "Christian" answer to that question. The Bible certainly suggests the wisdom of tithing. The Bible further suggests that our almsgiving is not to be accompanied by a fanfare of trumpets. Beyond that we are once again called upon to make a series of hard personal choices: What style of economic life most accords with my current sense of the call to discipleship?

Human relations are far too seldom thought of as an aspect of stewardship. Yet they are far more valuable than either our time or our money, and they are equally in need of caring attention. "Cultivating" friendships has sinister overtones. The phrase calls up ugly echoes of trying to win friends and influence people for purposes of self-aggrandizement. It might be less offensive to speak of weeding and fertilizing them—of pulling bitterness and hurt out by the roots, of adding such mundane ingredients as a letter or a phone call to help them grow. Both confrontation and comfort are essential to healthy friendships.

Family relations are equally in need of nurture, of course; but I have chosen the idiom of friendship because that language is currently being used with a new and helpful twist to empower our discipleship, and because that language offers, I think, the best analogy for the goal of our journey. As over against the long tradition which speaks of union with God as the goal, the term "friendship" suggests that we are to grow toward closer *communion*. Abraham, that model of one who set forth on a journey of faith, was called the friend of God (James 2:23). Jesus said to his disciples, when he told them to love one another, "You are my friends if you do what I command you" (John 15:14).

With contemporary revival of interest in Christian spirituality has come renewed interest in what is called "spiritual direction." A Christian on pilgrimage seeks out someone more experienced in the life of the spirit and asks for guidance. That person, lay or ordained, undertakes a close concern for the other's growth in the Christian life. Unfortunately, "spiritual director" suggests a hierarchical relationship. The other current terms, "spiritual friend" or "soul friend," bespeak, on the contrary, mutuality and intimacy and companionship in the Way—a shared adventure. In our stewardship, our responsible oversight, of our human relations, we all would be well served by such a friend with whom we could speak openly about the deepest wellsprings of our being.

It is a gift to be simple. The simplicity of life about which we have been thinking is shaped by a childlike wonder, one which Jürgen Moltmann calls the key to "the mysticism of everyday life." In *Experiences of God* he sums it up in one brief sentence: "Simple existence is life in God" (p. 76).

It is also a gift to be free. That Christian freedom of which Paul sang in his letter to the Galatians tells us that we do not have to observe "days, and months, and seasons, and years" in order to live Christian lives (Gal. 4:10). We do not have to be circumcised; we do not have to be slaves to any law. In the present context this means that there is no single pattern of life that deserves the label "Christian." The awesome gift of freedom entails God's approval of pluralism—of many different ways of shaping and ordering and disciplining our lives in response to God's gift of life.

There are also many different ways of praying. The wisdom of the ages says that each of us needs to adopt "A Rule of Life" if we are to grow up as praying people. In addition to a life-style that provides a climate for friendship with God, we need a special plan for learning to know God better and learning to love God more fully. But such a rule of life cannot come off the assembly line. It must be custom built.

To be sure, there are some basic ingredients. All of us need to read the Bible on our own, as well as to hear it read in church. All of us need to carve out some time and space each day to spend cultivating our friendship with God. All of us could profit by some other "spiritual reading" to learn from our forebears in the faith. All of us could well experiment with other time-tested practices of discipleship, such as periods of fasting and periods of retreat or withdrawal from everydayness, in order to pry ourselves open for the unexpected.

One traditional aid to spiritual growth that is currently being rediscovered is the practice of keeping a spiritual journal. Verbal people find it a helpful discipline to reflect in writing on their day-by-day journey with the Lord. A classic example of this form of spiritual exercise is the *Journal* of the eighteenth-century American Quaker John Woolman. Woolman's diary shows the deepening of his concern about slavery, the growth of his commitment to "a life so plain that little suffices." But perhaps the greatest insight that a modern Christian can gain from reading such a journal is that there are no small things in our lives. All that we do matters for God.

In the long run we each have to discover our own style of prayer, our own special vocabulary for converse with the One in whom we live and have our being. After analyzing the history of Christian spirituality, Urban Holmes emphasized this need for each of us to develop his or her own spiritual style. "What shape it takes will vary with each of us," he rightly insists (Holmes, *Introduction to the History of Christian Spirituality*, p. 158). We must each make the journey of the spirit in order to discover what is most natural for us.

Holmes identified two master images for that journey

from his survey of the Christian tradition—the desert and the mountain. Those images are closely related to what others have called the two ways—the Way of Negation and the Way of Affirmation, two routes for the pilgrimage. Both ways are amply charted in the literature of our spiritual heritage.

Anyone who has read the testimony of the desert fathers and mothers, listened to St. John of the Cross describe the dark night of the soul, or heard Moltmann talk about his encounters with God in his worst times as a prisoner of war must take the desert journey seriously. The Israelites wandered forty years in the wilderness on their way to the Promised Land. The Spirit drove Jesus into the wilderness for an equally symbolic forty days. The wilderness image speaks of the risk of Christian prayer. It reminds us that we will probably meet thorns and thistles and long periods of great dryness on our journey.

Mountain imagery does not suggest an easier trip. Anyone who has ever climbed up beyond the timberline carrying a heavy pack knows the difficulties involved. But mountain climbers also know the thrill of changing scenery, the unexpected mountain stream around a bend in the trail, the welcome level stretch after a particularly steep part of the ascent. They set out on the climb gladly, with good companions, anticipating adventure. Ultimately most of the climbers see the view from the top.

The Lord called to Moses from the top of Mt. Sinai, and Moses went up to meet the Lord. Jesus took three friends with him and led them up a high mountain, where God spoke to them also (Mark 9:2). Pilgrims traveling together up the road to Mt. Zion sang songs, psalms of ascent, to gladden their journey. With them we can affirm, "As the mountains are round about Jerusalem, so the LORD is round about his people" (Ps. 125:2). That Lord is the one who is always more ready to hear than we are ready to pray.

10

CENTERING DOWN

The substance of prayer, Simone Weil once said, is attention directed toward God. Paying attention demands keeping quiet and getting focused. The Quaker phrase for this kind of focus is "centering down." Before we say any more about what God wants to hear from us, we need to think about keeping quiet in order to hear from God.

Our culture is drowning in noise. It is surfeited with words. The constant wail of sirens, rumble of trucks, zoom of motorcycles, shrill of telephones assault our ears all day long. Alarm clocks wake us up and clock radios put many of us to sleep. We all know people who are almost terrified of silence, who cannot stand to be alone in a room without radio or television going. We also know compulsive talkers, people who do not dare be in the presence of another person without a spate of words to hide behind.

Such a culture cries out for the ministry of silence. It needs to learn again that silence is an indispensable discipline of the spiritual life. Our culture needs to discover as Elijah did that the voice of the Lord speaks most powerfully not in the great strong wind, nor in the roar of an earthquake, but in "a still small voice"—or, as the Hebrew literally says, in "a voice of silence" (I Kings 19:12).

To emphasize the need for silence in our search for God, Abraham Joshua Heschel quotes an anecdote from rab-

binic literature: "A certain reader once prayed in the presence of Rabbi Hanina and said, 'O God, the great, the
mighty, the revered, the majestic, the powerful, the
strong, the fearless, the all-wise, the certain, the honorable
. . .' Rabbi Hanina waited until he finished and then said
to him, 'Have you exhausted the praises of your Master?
Why do you say so much? . . . It is as if an earthly king had
a million denarii of gold, and we praised him for possessing
much silver.' " Heschel adds that with a different pointing
from that usually given the Hebrew text, Ps. 65:2 reads,
"To Thee, silence is praise" (Heschel, *Man's Quest for
God,* p. 43).

The silence in which prayer can be born, however, is
more than a matter of not talking, of not heaping up vain
words. It is not the silence of the lips that matters as much
as the silence of the heart. We can turn off the television,
go alone to a quiet spot, yet keep up a clamor of conversation with ourselves. What we need to learn to develop is
an inner stillness, one that can look at and listen to the
mystery which surrounds us. Then we need to surrender
to stillness, to relax and exhale and say yes to it.

Weil's word "attention" is a clue here. When we are
truly paying attention to something or someone, we are
not conscious of ourselves or our busy agendas. We do not
think about all the things we have to accomplish tomorrow
or about all the things we did not get done today. We are
not silently making out our grocery lists or deciding what
to say as soon as the other person stops talking. We are
wholly absorbed.

John V. Taylor retells the story of a woman who had
prayed for fourteen years without ever sensing the presence of God. Then one day she went to her room, sat down
in a comfortable chair, and started knitting. She felt
relaxed and contented. She noticed with pleasure the familiar view through the window, the familiar furniture,
the familiar clicking of her knitting needles. Gradually she

became aware that the silence around her was not an empty one. In her words: "The silence around began to come and meet the silence in me. . . . All of a sudden I perceived that the silence was a presence. At the heart of the silence there was Him."

Awareness of God's presence came in this instance through relaxed awareness of pleasant everyday surroundings. The story is an excellent example of the immanence of God, of his presence in and through the things which he has made. We meet God in the midst of the commonplace.

Michel Quoist makes a similar affirmation of the immanence of God. He says that if we knew how to listen to God and if we knew how to look at life, all life would become a sign and all life would become prayer. Quoist uses his unblinded eyes and opened ears to meet God in the subway. He hears God speak from green blackboards and sees him in a twenty-dollar bill, a bald head, a wire fence—all because he is convinced that even the smallest things are gifts from God. He thinks that God *is* speaking to us; we have only to listen. He thinks that if we look at life as God sees it, we will discover that nothing is secular (Quoist, *Prayers*).

The quality of attention that enables us to hear and see God at work in and through the commonplace is closely allied with a childlike wonder, with what might be described as the gift of innocence or, more accurately, with what Albert Einstein called a holy curiosity. Holy curiosity is a gift that can be exercised in your own backyard.

No one has celebrated this gift better than the young American writer Annie Dillard in her prizewinning book, *Pilgrim at Tinker Creek*. She has much to teach us about attention, about centering down. She looks at things— really looks. At a sycamore tree, at a dying frog, at the light in a cedar tree. She listens to a mockingbird and wonders *why* it sings. She even *feels* things with holy curiosity—

pats a beagle puppy at the filling station in awed wonder, working her hand over its fur, following the line of hair under its ears and along the hot-skinned belly.

Dillard consciously practices the art of curiosity, although I doubt that she would feel comfortable with the assertion that she thereby practices the presence of God. She keeps a microscope on her kitchen shelf. She uses it to look at a drop of duck pond water brought home from a springtime walk and spread on a glass slide—trying to look spring in the eye. The microscope at her forehead, she says, is a kind of phylactery, that ancient Jewish symbol of prayer and praise. She is seeking to live fully in the present, with concentration and with receptiveness.

Consciously or unconsciously, this modern pilgrim exhibits what John Macquarrie calls Celtic spirituality. The Celtic monk was a God-intoxicated person with an intense sense of God's presence mediated through the stuff of creation. Because he sensed God's presence in nature so strongly, he was always in danger of pantheism. But he also sensed God's presence in the trivial round, the common tasks of daily life indoors. Getting out of bed, lighting the fire, cooking breakfast were all occasions for recognizing the presence of God. One is reminded of Brother Lawrence, though he was not a Celt but a seventeenth-century native of Lorraine, scrubbing his pots and pans to the glory of God.

God is always present with us, we have been saying. We need only to pay attention to that presence. Such a deliberate act of attention can take the form of a focused silence, wherein we relax and wait and listen. It can take the form of a focused expectancy, wherein we look and wonder. Or it can take the form of an added dimension in our everyday chores. We can meet God in our bedrooms or in our backyards, in our offices or in our kitchens. We have only to stop to look, stop to listen, stop to wonder, stop to pray.

Two brief sentences in the Bible sum up the attitude of the centered-down person waiting on God, the attitude we have been talking about. They call for our focused attention in the remainder of this chapter. The first is from Isaiah: "Here am I!" (Isa. 6:8). The second is from Luke: "Let it be to me according to your word" (Luke 1:38).

"Here am I!" Isaiah said this to God in the Temple in Jerusalem during his profound experience of God's majesty, at a time when he was deeply disturbed by the shaking of the foundations of his nation and by his own personal questions about his vocation. His whole vision of the Holy One of Israel, recounted in Isaiah 6, is a virtually inexhaustible paradigm of authentic prayer and worship. But at present just those three words are enough to think about.

The point of centering down, however and wherever we attempt to do it, is not only to recognize God's constant presence with us. It is also to make ourselves present to God. Simply, quietly, unreservedly to say, "Here am I!"

Our experience of friendship can again help us here. I remember vividly the strong presence of a friend at the time of my father's death. I called. He came. I don't remember what he said, or whether he said anything. He was just there. Everyone has similar memories of a personal presence, of someone being with you and for you. God is the one who always comes to be with us, on this analogy. God does not need our sustaining presence. But God does want our availability, our putting ourselves at his disposal. God wants us to say, "Here am I!"

That kind of total presence to the Other does not depend on our first getting all dressed up and ready for a royal audience. The sentimental old hymn is correct in that respect: "Just as I am, without one plea." Prayer is indeed a come-as-you-are party. Nor does it depend on our first clearing off the desk or polishing off the dishes. Jesus told a powerful parable about the plausible excuses we think up for refusing his invitation to come to his party. We share a common, universal tendency to say, "I pray you, have me excused" (Luke 14:16–24). But God wants us to say, "Here am I!"

The simplicity of Isaiah's "Here am I!" is akin to a child's when that child has been away for a while, perhaps half an hour, and then storms in the back door shouting: "I'm home! I'm home!" There is a profound trust in that announcement of presence. The child takes for granted that the parents are glad to know that their offspring is home again. And so they are. And so is God.

The other biblical sentence that serves as a summary for what happens in silence before God is Mary's simple, "Let it be to me according to your word." Taken by itself as an all-sufficient model for Christian spirituality, that sentence can have dangerous consequences. It can lead to an unhealthy kind of quietism, one determined to thank God for everything that happens in the world, including all suffering and darkness and evil. This is an old theme of Christian piety. It is summed up in the advice given by the eighteenth-century English clergyman William Law. He made it a rule that one should praise and thank God for everything that happens, every calamity that befalls one. One thereby turns it into a blessing, he said. As I shall assert in the next chapter, such a blanket acquiescence to everything defuses responsible Christian freedom.

By the same token, Mary's be-it-unto-me response, especially when internalized by women, can lead to a neurotic doormat attitude toward life. Feminist critics of the Christian tradition such as Phyllis Chesler have argued that it can lead, indeed, directly to madness. She believes that too many women have looked to Mary as a model and thereby negated their own God-given individuality, their own strong personhood. They have said be-it-unto-me not only to God but to every male figure in their lives.

Such extreme reactions to Mary's yes to God miss the

tough responsiveness of her corollary to Isaiah's "Here am I!" She simply opened herself to God. Such an offering of the self to God from the stillness of an attentive heart is always a response to the initiative of God the Spirit. It is an answer to God's prior word. It reflects that silence before the Word which Bonhoeffer well described as "humble stillness." It accepts what Nouwen calls "the divine silence in which love rests secure."

When Mary said her world-changing yes to God, she did so in the midst of an ordinary, unspectacular life in a provincial town with no claims to fame. If we accept Luke's portrait of her, she subsequently protested her son's seemingly thoughtless behavior even as she pondered in her heart the meaning of what was happening to her. The silence of Mary was not a dumb silence. She had things well in focus. She was paying attention. She was a woman fully centered down. And because of that, she was enabled to become bearer of the Word.

11

THE VOCABULARY OF PRAYER

Out of the silence comes a word of presence. In God's presence we seek to become more fully the persons we were created to be, slowly, patiently, always resisting the urge to pull ourselves up by the roots to see how well we are growing. We seek to become more childlike in our trust of God's good purpose for our lives.

Children sometimes have enormous vocabularies by the time they are ready for nursery school. If parents have done their job well, there are at least three words they have learned to use regularly as evidence that they are socialized creatures: "please," "thank you," and "I'm sorry." A fourth word all children somehow discover by the time they are two. For many months they use it incessantly—the word "why?" These four words constitute a basic vocabulary of prayer for all ages. We will think about them in this chapter, starting with the last.

Many people have never discovered that "Why?" has a legitimate place in praying. Pamphlets on how to pray seldom include it. Yet it is one of our most basic, most persistent, and sometimes most agonizing religious questions. Why, God, do you allow thousands of children to starve to death in East Africa? Why, Lord, can't you stop the senseless violence in our world? Why, oh, why did this have to happen to my child? my family? me?

These are truly prayers of the heart. If we are to be honest in our friendship, we must address them to God—not just to the chaplain in the hospital or to ourselves in the dark of the night. If anyone has doubts about that, a quick reading of the Book of Job is recommended. Far from being the proverbial patient man, Job is one of the most impatient in all literature. He is insistent in his questioning. He demands that God answer him. Why?

Or consider Jeremiah, that much-afflicted servant of God. He asks why he was ever born, why he was ever recruited for the thankless job of prophet. He wants nothing more than to get off into the country on vacation. Oh, that I had a place to escape to. Why me, Lord?

The psalms are equally punctuated with question marks. Why do the righteous suffer, while the wicked are so prosperous? "O God, why have you utterly cast us off? Why is your wrath so hot against the sheep of your pasture?" (Ps. 74:1). We have good scriptural basis for shaking our fists in God's face, as it were, for confronting God with our deepest questions. Why?

If we have learned to be still before God, we have discovered that in his caring presence we are free to talk our lives over fully. The lives of most of us are pervaded with doubts and uncertainties, with frustrations and furies. No one who reads the daily newspaper can sing Pippa's refrain: "God's in his heaven—All's right with the world!" We need to be passionate people in our prayer.

Søren Kierkegaard, that strange Danish Christian, campaigned vigorously for such honesty before God. Opposed to the easy, bland and respectable middle-class Christendom of the Established Church, he wanted to bring Christ urgently alive for the individual. "Passion is the real thing, the real measure of man's power," he noted in his *Journal* of 1841, "and the age in which we live is wretched because it is without passion."

Kierkegaard was against what he called "unshaven passion," however. He sought a purified passion, a troubled truth. In one of his journal entries, he gives us a glimpse of what that meant for his own life of prayer: "He lets me weep before him in silent solitude, pour forth and again pour forth my pain, with the blessed consolation of knowing that he is concerned for me—and in the meanwhile he gives that life of pain a significance which almost overwhelms me, gives me good fortune and strength and wisdom for my whole undertaking."

The contemporary German theologian Johann Metz, in a brief essay on *The Courage to Pray,* thinks that we must not be overly affirmative in our prayers. He believes that this just leads to a dangerous apathy. We need to express our pain and the suffering of the world around us. "The language of prayer is that of our impassioned questioning of God," he writes. Indeed, "prayer is really an act of opposition," one that resists the dehumanizing forces in society. It must stir us up. Courageous prayer has political consequences.

The second fundamental word in the lexicon of prayer is the word "sorry." Yet that English word does not convey the depths of self-recognition that occur in the presence of the Holy God. Metz speaks of the prayer of guilt, and suggests that such prayer can free us from the net of excuses we weave around ourselves. The spontaneous reaction of Isaiah when he found himself before God captures this kind of prayer in full force: "Woe is me! For I am lost; for I am a man of unclean lips, and I dwell in the midst of a people of unclean lips" (Isa. 6:5).

Corporate confession of sin is a normal part of most Sunday worship, but I have reserved discussion of it until now because the word of confession must first be said in the first person singular before it can be transposed into the plural, as Isaiah's outcry indicates. I am guilty of not loving God with my whole heart. I am guilty of not loving my neighbor as myself. So are you. That is why we to·

gether can acknowledge our sin, even if we are no longer willing to use the archaic language and call ourselves "miserable offenders." And we ask for forgiveness.

Prayer of confession is made possible by our knowledge of what God is like. The love made known to us through Jesus Christ is a love which seeks the lost. It is a love which takes the initiative to call us home again. As Reinhold Niebuhr once said, the final form of love is forgiveness.

The so-called parable of the prodigal son might better be called the parable of the forgiving father. It presents us with the most vivid picture of forgiveness in all of Scripture. While the son was on his way home but still a long way off, "his father saw him and had compassion, and ran and embraced him and kissed him" (Luke 15:20). Forgiveness is not of sins but of persons. It restores us to a relationship that had been broken. We cannot restore ourselves.

Prayer of confession is made necessary by our recognition of our own lostness—our alienation and estrangement from ourselves and our neighbors and from God. We know ourselves to be responsible for the broken relationships. What the Christian confesses is not in the first instance sins, but sin—the state of sin which is lovelessness, rather than sins as deliberate acts against conscience, the things done and left undone which are individual blows to a loving heart.

But prayer of confession is a great good gift because it meets our deepest need. "Ultimately, every person needs someone whom he cannot fool," a wise priest once wrote. We spend a good deal of time and energy trying to fool ourselves and those around us into believing that we are acceptable people. Only rarely do we trust someone enough to tell that person the uncomfortable, unflattering truth about ourselves. God is the only one who can never be fooled. God already knows us thoroughly—and knowing, cares. So we are free to take off our masks and be ourselves, sure of his judgment and mercy.

The judgment is real. God is not a flabby grandfather. David Head, in his book *He Sent Leanness,* parodied the confession of those who think that God's mercy is automatic: "Do thou, O Lord, deal lightly with our infrequent lapses. Be thy own sweet Self with those who admit they are not perfect; According to the unlimited tolerance which we have a right to expect from thee. And grant as an indulgent Parent that we may hereafter continue to live a harmless and happy life and keep our self-respect" (p. 19).

Forgiveness is not saying "it doesn't matter." Sin does matter. We need to be blamed when we know that we are blameworthy. The noted psychiatrist Karl Menninger recognized that deep psychic need in his call for the revival of the good old-fashioned term, under the title *Whatever Became of Sin?* Some people are indeed troubled with neurotic guilt feelings, but many more of us have real guilt feelings. We need to say, "I'm sorry." Only confession and assurance of forgiveness can free us to turn around and start afresh. So confession is a healing gift, just as forgiveness is a costly one—one given from the cross.

"Please" is the third word in the primer of prayer. It applies equally to what are classically called petition and intercession, prayer for self and prayer for others; but I want to postpone discussing intercession to the next chapter. Here we will think only about asking for things— physical and spiritual—for ourselves. In spite of a heavy weight of misguided tradition which equates such prayer with selfishness, Jesus evidently thought it was a good thing.

More than any of the other Evangelists, Luke cherishes Jesus' teaching about prayer. Three parables on the subject are found only in Luke's Gospel. With refreshing bluntness, Frederick Buechner calls two of them jokes. It is thanks to Luke, he reports, that we know "about the man who kept knocking at his friend's door till he finally got out of bed to open it and the widow who kept bugging the crooked judge till he finally heard her case just to get a little peace" (*Peculiar Treasures,* p. 94). More formal scholarship calls the first of these parables "the friend at midnight" (Luke 11:5–8) and the second "the parable of the unjust judge" (Luke 18:1–5). The third special Lucan parable on prayer follows immediately. It is about the Pharisee and the tax collector (Luke 18:9–14).

Buechner thinks that the first two parables share a common point—"if you don't think that God heard you the first time, keep on until you are hoarse." Perhaps; but a closer look can tell us more about the way in which we are invited to present our petitions to the Lord. On first reading they seem to say merely that God will give in to our requests so that we won't bother him anymore.

It is noteworthy that a man is pounding on the door in the first story and a woman in the second. Perhaps the two parables were originally told at the same time. Luke often records twin parables, addressed to male and female. He presents Jesus as a rabbi who was consciously drawing all his listeners into the parabolic world.

The first illustration now follows directly on Luke's version of the Lord's Prayer. The parable uses the language of friendship. One friend comes to another in the middle of the night to borrow some bread for an unexpected guest. The sleepy householder is not willing to get up just because a friend is at the door, but he eventually drags himself out because his friend does not give up and go home. After this parable Luke inserts an originally separate saying of Jesus, telling us to ask, to seek, and to knock.

The second story has a woman coming time after time to a judge to demand that he hear her case. Neither this story nor the preceding one is an allegory. The judge who does not care about anyone but himself is manifestly not to be thought of as God. Rather, we are meant to identify with the persistent widow, even though we are given no details about her legal problem. Her active badgering of the judge brings results.

You will have noticed that neither of these funny stories is a very good illustration of politely saying "please." They both come closer to that begging use of "Please!" we overhear in the grocery store when a child is pleading with mother for a candy bar. Yet Jesus, while making his listeners laugh at themselves, also encourages them to take action, to take the initiative on their own behalf. Part of the power of parables, as of laughter, is to energize people for action. Luke says that Jesus told the story about the widow "to the effect that they ought always to pray and not lose heart" (Luke 18:1). It is the action of prayer rather than the content of the request that matters most.

We may legitimately pray for anything that we need or want. All such prayer is answered, even if sometimes the answer is "no." Such prayer is a kind of exploration, a seeking to discover God's will—without making up our minds too quickly or too firmly as to what that will might be. The essential element in such petition is the lively dialogue with the God who made us for responsive freedom. With masterful understatement Luke pictures the opposite kind of prayer in the next parable. "The Pharisee stood and prayed thus with himself" (Luke 18:11).

Finally, "thank you." The core of corporate Christian worship, we have argued, is Eucharist. So, too, is the heart of personal prayer. Because we gather on Sunday morning to give thanks, we are challenged to punctuate the other six days of the week with thanksgiving also—to point them up and mark them with gratitude. This does not mean trying to learn to play Pollyanna's "Glad Game," fatuously looking always on the bright side of life. Nor does it mean, as should be clear from what has been said about questioning God, that we passively accept as God's will whatever comes. Rather, it means the active response of the open-eyed.

The trinitarian theology of worship with which we started our study can help focus our thinking about this fourth voice of prayer. Human spirits inbreathed by Holy Spirit are empowered to see God at work in unexpected places and in unexpected people. It is a spiritual gift to discover unitive Being at work in a committee meeting, helping people reach a consensus. It is a spiritual gift when an overworked salesperson really looks at you and smiles. Simply and naturally we can practice saying thank you for such gifts to the Lord, who is the Spirit.

Human beings who know themselves to be sons and daughters of God, in Christ, are likewise enabled to give thanks for God's "inestimable love in the redemption of the world by our Lord Jesus Christ," as an old prayer puts it. That includes thanks for the capacity to get up and start again after we fall flat on our faces in failure. It includes giving thanks for all other human beings, for whom Christ also died, however difficult this may sometimes be in practice when we do not feel particularly thankful for the driver who is poking along in front of us or for the landlord who has just raised the rent.

Creatures, made in the image of God, can further learn to rejoice in God's whole creation. This dimension of thankfulness is the first cousin of the kind of wondering attention that Annie Dillard exemplifies. It is "our humble answer to the inconceivable surprise of living" (Heschel).

Poets can sometimes open our eyes to behold God's gracious hand in all the world as well or better than priests. But Michel Quoist, who is in fact both, thanks God for "the water that woke me up, the soap that smells good, the toothpaste that refreshes." He continues in his observant catalog of daily graces to say thank you for the gas that made his car carry him meekly where he wanted to go, for the glass of beer at lunch, for the friend who gave him a cigarette, for the person who held the door open for him. He thanks the Lord for life (Quoist, *Prayers,* pp. 62–63).

We all have our own personal catalogs of thanksgiving for the gifts of creation, and it is helpful from time to time to write them down. Mine includes such items as the smell of sun on pine needles and of bacon frying, the feel of a baby's skin, Handel's "Water Music," the Grand Tetons. And, oddly, the dustballs under my bed. Gerard Manley Hopkins, the nineteenth-century English poet-priest, had a preference for "dappled things": "All things counter, original, spare, strange." He responded in thankful wonder to "all trades, their gear and tackle and trim." The opening line of another of his poems sums up the cause and occasion of our saying thank you: "The world is charged with the grandeur of God." Because we live in that kind of sacramental universe, we inhabit a web of glory.

12

THE WEB OF GLORY

Forty years ago a group of friends used to gather on Tuesdays at the Bird and Baby Pub in Oxford to drink beer together. On Thursdays they gathered again in the Magdalen College rooms of one of the group and exchanged stories and ideas. J. R. R. Tolkien, who was one of the friends, said of those Thursdays, "That was true joy!"

Because all these friends were gifted writers, they have left us some powerful images. Because they were all Christians, they can help to school our imaginations. Two of these Oxford Christians coined phrases which I want to consider in this final chapter. Charles Williams is author of the term "the web of glory." C. S. Lewis summed up his central life experience in the words "surprised by joy."

On Williams' gravestone in St. Cross Churchyard, Oxford, is inscribed: "Poet. Under the Mercy." He is better known in this country, however, not for his difficult poetry but for his novels of the supernatural and for his history of the church, *The Descent of the Dove,* which W. H. Auden called his masterpiece. The history maps clearly the Way of Affirmation through the centuries. The novels bring to life his vision of a web of glory that is upheld by the way of exchange, the way of substitution.

People who do not like spiders are sometimes put off by the image of a web; but anyone who has encountered a

complete spider's web on some early-morning walk, especially one still beaded with dew, has an indelible picture
of an engineering marvel. The crisscross of delicate
strands that hold each other up combine in a pattern of
great beauty and of great toughness. This for Williams is
the image from which God's Kingdom shines forth, woven
through interchange. You and I are called, he believed, to
become strands in that web, to become "one of the living
creatures which compose the web of glory."

Williams was well aware that the idea of praying for
others poses difficulties for the contemporary intellect. He
was also well aware that we don't much enjoy being
prayed *for*, either. He knew how hard it is to be grateful
for "the smirk of well-meaning intercession by the official
twice-born in the visible Church." Given Williams' understanding of the activity of intercession, however, the
whole concept becomes not verbal but vital.

Paul provided the key text that informed this extraordinary Christian's theory of the way of exchange and his
distinctive theology of substituted love. "Bear one another's burdens," Paul wrote to the Galatians, "and so fulfil
the law of Christ" (Gal. 6:2). Charles Williams believed
that this injunction literally describes the way things work
in God's universe.

The theme of exchange pervades all seven of Williams'
novels, but the most explicit discussion of it comes in a
conversation between a young woman named Pauline and
an artist named Peter Stanhope in *Descent Into Hell.* Pauline is haunted by fears and by the fear of fear. Peter
simply offers to carry those fears for her. He quotes Paul
on the subject, and rightly guesses that she thinks the text
just means listening sympathetically. But Peter claims that
it means something much more like carrying a parcel for
someone else.

"To bear a burden is precisely to carry it instead of," he
says. "If you're still carrying yours, I'm not carrying it for

you—however sympathetic I may be. And anyhow there's no need to introduce Christ, unless you wish. It's a fact of experience. If you give a weight to me, you can't be carrying it yourself; all I'm asking you to do is to notice that blazing truth."

In *He Came Down from Heaven,* a theological essay which Williams dedicated to his wife, Michal, "by whom I began to study the doctrine of glory," Williams explains that this action of exchange needs practice and intelligence. Even though it is the commerce of love between friends, it is much like any other business contract. Three steps are required: knowing the burden, giving up the burden, and taking up the burden. The hardest step is giving up the burden. Although we talk glibly of casting our burdens on the Lord, we are reluctant to hand them over to anyone else. But you cannot carry my suitcase unless I let go of it.

Such very concrete and intentional exchanges are normal in the web of glory. They are exchanges between consenting adults. Williams was much opposed to what he called emotional bullying, and therefore he insisted that the best way to practice powerful intercession is with the knowledge and consent of those whose burdens we would carry. Nevertheless, he acknowledged that more general intercessory prayer also has a place in the web of glory. It cannot be dangerous to present all pains and distresses to the Kingdom, he said.

All pains and distresses, however, share in the scandal of particularity which is part of the Christian gospel. One fitting method of intercessory prayer therefore uses the daily newspaper as a guide. The aim is to focus on the realities of human need and human suffering there reported, consciously holding them within the web whose center and circumference are the love of God. Although very few of us have grown far enough in the life of faith to manage this kind of prayerful attention to every item

in the daily newspaper, we discover in the process of trying this method that certain pains and distresses have, as
it were, our names attached. In the design of God, it
seems, some of us are called to intercede especially, say,
for peace in the Middle East, while others are assigned to
pay attention to South Africa. The web of exchange stretches around the globe. Some Christians in Tehran or Cape-
town may be praying right now for people in Atlanta.

After Pope John Paul II was shot in an assassination
attempt, a young man who seldom goes near a church
wandered into St. Patrick's Cathedral in New York City.
Although the secular world as represented by the mass
media seemed at a loss to know how to behave in the face
of such a grave crisis, he later declared, the people he
found in St. Patrick's were not. All sorts and conditions of
people were there—praying. The young man's own experience there is a notable example of the embodied con-
tours of Christian intercession. Sitting in a back pew, he
found himself thinking, he said, not about what the global
consequences of the attack might be, nor even about "the
pope." Rather, he found himself thinking about Karol
Wojtyla, the wounded person lying on an operating table
in a hospital in Rome.

Two major theological premises undergird Charles Williams' notion of the way of exchange. He was convinced
that the cross of Christ is the paradigm for the doctrine of
substituted love. The new life that Christ came to give so
abundantly, he argued, began with substitution and proceeds with substitution. That is why Paul could end his
admonition to bear one another's burdens with the clause,
"And so fulfil the law of Christ." The taunt to our Lord on
the cross, "He saved others, himself he cannot save," was
for Williams a precise definition of the Kingdom of
Heaven in operation. He was also convinced that the doctrine of the Trinity helps us to recognize the fact that
coinherence is the hallmark of ultimate reality. For God

is himself, as he put it, One working in the others.

The triune God whom Christians worship, we said in the first chapter, is not a god who sits still in whatever niche of the temple his priests shelve him. He is God on the move, God blowing wherever he wills, God casting down the mighty from their seats and raising up those of low degree. He is therefore the God of our complete surprising. Both in corporate prayer and in individual worship we are in the presence of the Lord of the unexpected.

Charles Williams' Oxford friend C. S. Lewis captured this fact of Christian experience with supreme accuracy in the title of his autobiography, *Surprised by Joy.* Lewis was best known in England as the don who introduced Christianity to the BBC through his radio talks, making a strong case for the truth of the faith. He is probably best known in this country for the television version of his Narnia chronicle, *The Lion, the Witch, and the Wardrobe.* He knew himself as one grasped by that for which he longed, but which he never really believed could happen.

The joy about which Lewis was talking is the very antithesis of cotton candy. It has no cloying sugar taste about it. Indeed, it was for him bittersweet and fleeting. It first came upon him while he was riding in that most ordinary vehicle—a public bus. Yet it surprised Lewis into lucid certitude that God's love had laid claim upon him. And that joyous surprise turned him into one of this century's most powerful apostles to skeptics. It also turned him into a man who knelt daily to pray.

Worship can be a perilous activity. That we have acknowledged. But worship is also a way of becoming more fully human. Through the shared public liturgy of our Sundays and the shared private prayer of our Mondays we grow in the joy of freedom. That is the joy with which God surprises those who seek him in spirit and in truth.

QUESTIONS FOR REFLECTION
AND DISCUSSION

Part One. A THEOLOGY OF WORSHIP

1. What forms of idolatry do you see around you? To what kind of idolatry are you yourself most tempted?

2. Which do you think is the more serious danger in worship today—overenthusiasm or lukewarmness? Why?

3. What kinds of power do you expect from worship? What sorts of power have you experienced in worship?

4. How do you see God the Spirit at work building community in your congregation? How do you express community in your worship together?

5. How do you honestly think your congregation would respond to the sermon that Jesus preached in the synagogue at Nazareth, according to Luke 4:16ff.?

6. What images of fatherhood do you associate with the Lord's Prayer?

7. How do you interpret the petition of the Lord's Prayer that is traditionally translated, "lead us not into temptation"?

8. Think about the ways in which you use each of your five senses in worship. What use do you make of your eyes and ears? To what extent and in what specific ways do you also use your sense of smell? Of touch? Of taste?

9. What difference, if any, would it make to your wor-

ship if you believed (or disbelieved) that other spiritual creatures, such as angels, were also worshiping with you?

10. How much diversity in worship are you personally comfortable with? How does your understanding of God affect your thinking about that question?

Part Two. THE BODY AT WORSHIP

1. How do you spend Sunday when you are on vacation? Is the quality of the day different from Sundays when you are not on vacation? If so, how and why? If not, why not?

2. What kind of symbolic language does the building in which you worship speak? What does the space "say" about what you are doing and why?

3. Do you think your congregation should choose just one translation of the Bible to read in public worship or several? What difference does it make?

4. Do you routinely look at your watch at the start of a sermon? How would you describe the way you listen to sermons? Are you curious, critical, docile, receptive, or what?

5. Would your experience of worship be different if you never participated in the Lord's Supper? How?

6. What do you think about the claim that "picketing is a form of praying" and "praying is a form of picketing"?

7. Can you name your favorite hymn? What makes it your favorite?

8. Imagine that your congregation decided to institute a version of the biblical footwashing in your regular Sunday services? What advantages and disadvantages might it have?

9. When you go home from Sunday worship, do you think any more or talk about the service? What kinds of things do you or could you think or talk about?

10. How is Monday related to Sunday in your actual

experience? How is Sunday related to Monday in your own Christian theology?

Part Three. PRAYING PEOPLE

1. What are your most serious problems with the tyranny of time? How could you best claim more of it to spend freely however you chose to?

2. Have you ever had a relationship with a "spiritual director" or "spiritual friend"? If so, what was it like? If not, what do you think of the idea?

3. Does the metaphor of "the desert" or "the mountain" better describe the landscape of your own spiritual journey? Or is there another more adequate image?

4. How much silence are you comfortable with? How does the distinction between an "empty" and a "filled" silence make a difference in your answer?

5. Where and under what circumstances are you most aware of the presence of God?

6. What three "why" questions would you most like to address to God today?

7. What do you think is the difference between forgiving and forgetting?

8. For what single gift of creation are you most thankful today? For what gift of human manufacture?

9. What do you think happens when you pray for someone you know? How do you feel when you are being prayed for?

10. What was the last time you were really and truly surprised? How did you feel?

REFERENCES

The following modern works were cited in the text:

Brueggemann, Walter. *Living Toward a Vision.* United Church Press, 1976.

Buechner, Frederick. *Peculiar Treasures: A Biblical Who's Who.* Harper & Row, 1979.

Cone, James H. *The Spirituals and the Blues.* Seabury Press, 1972.

Dillard, Annie. *Pilgrim at Tinker Creek.* Bantam Books, 1975.

Head, David. *He Sent Leanness: A Book of Prayers for the Natural Man.* Macmillan Co., 1959.

Heschel, Abraham Joshua. *Man's Quest for God.* Charles Scribner's Sons, 1954.

Holmes, Urban T., III. *Introduction to the History of Christian Spirituality.* Seabury Press, 1980.

Moltmann, Jürgen. *Experiences of God.* Fortress Press, 1980.

Nouwen, Henri. *Reaching Out: Three Movements of Spiritual Life.* Doubleday & Co., 1975.

Quoist, Michel. *Prayers.* Sheed & Ward, 1963.

Rahner, Karl, and Metz, Johann. *The Courage to Pray.* Seabury Press, Crossroad Book, 1980.

Tillich, Paul. *Systematic Theology,* Vol. III. University of Chicago Press, 1963.

DATE DUE